BIGGEST BOOK OF QUIZZES

Kidsbooks®

Visit us at www.kidsbooks.com

Multiple Choice,
**True or False,
This or That,
and More!**

Do you think you know all there is to know about sports, animals, fashion, history, and more? Get ready for hours of fun as you to test your knowledge and learn fascinating facts with

The Biggest Book of Quizzes!

Whether you're a boy or a girl, you will enjoy learning about a wide variety of subjects through Multiple Choice, True or False, Fill in the Blank, This or That, and many more types of quizzes. And, you'll be sure to impress friends, family, and teachers with all that you've learned along the way!

So, grab a pencil or pen and get ready for some fun!

Kidsbooks®

Where's your **VACATION** destination?

Are you a **SPORTS FANATIC?**

What type of **MUSIC** do you like?

Can you keep a **SECRET?**

A DOG'S LIFE

How well do you know dogs? Find out by marking each statement either "True" or "False." Then, check your answers.

	TRUE	FALSE
1. The bulldog is the most popular breed of dog in the world.	○	✓
2. Dogs can detect scents thousands of times less concentrated than humans can.	✓	○
3. All dogs bark.	○	✓
4. Greyhounds have been known to run upward of forty miles per hour.	✓	○
5. The oldest dog in history was a Queensland heeler who lived to be 29 years old.	✓	○
6. Poodles were first bred in France.	○	✓

7. Small breeds, like the Pekingese, were first bred in China by skilled trainers.

8. Some experts believe that dogs were the very first domesticated animals.

9. Dogs sweat.

10. About a third of all Dalmatians born are deaf either in one or both ears.

Answers

1. False. The Labrador retriever is the most popular breed. Varieties of this breed include yellow, black, and chocolate.

2. True.

3. False. The Basenji, an African breed, "yodels" rather than barks.

4. True.

5. True.

6. False. The word "poodle" relates to the German word pudel, or splashing dog. Poodles are excellent swimmers.

7. True.

8. True.

9. False. Dogs cool themselves by panting and maintaining a wet, cool nose.

10. True.

Test Your Animal Knowledge

Test your animal knowledge by reading the questions and taking a guess at the answers!

Q: Sharks continually replace lost teeth. About how many teeth can a shark grow in a lifetime?

A: 24,000

Q: What type of bird eats with its bill upside down?

A: The flamingo

Q: What is the only insect that can turn its head from side to side without moving its body?

A: The praying mantis, which can turn its head more than 180 degrees to either side.

Q: What is the only kind of cat that can't retract its claws?

A: The cheetah

Q: What do all insects have in common?

A: All insects have six legs.

Q: Do turtles have teeth?

A: No, but the edges of their jaws can be razor-sharp.

Q: What kind of whale was Moby Dick?

A: A sperm whale

Q: Which type of mosquito bites us: the male only, the female only, or both?

A: The female only

Q: Not counting queen ants, how long is an ant's life span?

A: 8 to 10 weeks (A queen ant can live as long as 15 years.)

Are You a Music Fanatic?

1. The school dance is coming up! What are you most excited about?
- **A.** Getting dressed up and hanging out with friends.
- **B.** Dancing, of course!
- **C.** Having the DJ play a list of my favorite songs!

2. Do you play a musical instrument?
- **A.** I always wanted to try...
- **B.** I do, but I should probably practice more.
- **C.** Just one? I play a few!

3. Your favorite artist is releasing a new album tomorrow. What do you do?
- **A.** I'll probably pick it up in a few days.
- **B.** Order it online the day it comes out.
- **C.** Beg my parents to let me wait outside the music store the night before it arrives!

4. All the speaking parts in the school play are taken. You get a part in the chorus—how do you feel?
- **A.** A little disappointed.
- **B.** The chorus should be fun, but a speaking part would've been nice.
- **C.** Perfect!

5. Do you sing in the shower?
- **A.** Sure...sometimes.
- **B.** Yes, why not?
- **C.** There are people who don't sing in the shower?

Mostly A's

You're Just Starting Out!

So you're interested in music, but you just haven't found something you're really into. No problem! Try expanding your horizons—if you make a point to listen to all different styles of music, you're bound to find something that you'll tap your feet to.

Mostly B's

On Your Way to Being a True Fan

Music plays a big part in your life. You definitely have some styles and artists you like, and you aren't afraid to try new things, too. Your tastes will change for sure, but music is something you'll always love!

Mostly C's

Music is Your Life!

Wow, you are a true audiophile! You've got most people beat when it comes to loving music, and it shows. Whether it's taking in some new tunes or showing off your own musical talent, no one can match your musical obsession!

Horsing Around

Test out your horse knowledge with this quiz! The letter of each answer corresponds to a blank in the secret message at the end of the quiz. Get the answers right to uncover the message!

1. What do you call a young, female horse?

N. a pup

O. a filly

P. a colt

Q. a foal

2. What unit of measure do you use to measure a horse's height?

U. hand

V. foot

W. knee

X. inch

3. What does a horse use its tail for?

Q. to help it run

R. to shade its legs

S. to signal to other horses

T. to shoo away bugs

4. What do horses sometimes wear on their heads?

G. squinters

H. masks

I. blinders

J. hats

5. What do you call the offspring of a horse and a donkey?

C. a zedonk

D. a mule

E. a stallion

F. a mare

Answers

1. (O) A filly is a young female horse. A colt is a young male horse, a foal is a baby horse, male or female, and a pup is a baby dog or seal.

2. (U) A "hand" isn't an exact unit. It is usually the same as four inches.

3. (T) A horse uses its tail to shoo away bugs. Some horse owners will braid their horse's tail—some even use ribbons!

4. (I) The blinders keep a horse from seeing to the side, something that may help it keep calm while in crowds.

5. (D) A mule is a cross between a horse and a donkey!

Which side of a horse has the most hair?

THE __ __ __ S __ __ E
(1) (2) (3)   (4) (5)

Answer: THE OUTSIDE

Once Upon a Time

Everyone loves a good fairy tale! Can you tell which fairy tale character is which from the clues below?

Cinderella • Goldilocks • Hansel • Jack, from Jack and the Beanstalk • Little Red Riding Hood • Rapunzel • Robin Hood • Snow White • The Frog Prince • The Little Mermaid

1. Pretending you are someone you're not is no joke! All I was trying to do was visit my sick grandmother in my neat, fashionable cape and I find out someone's broken in to her house . Good thing that lumberjack was there to save me. **Who am I?**

_____

2. All I do every day is work, work, work. My stepsisters are SO mean. My fairy godmother says she'll get me to the big dance tomorrow, but all she has to work with is an oversized pumpkin and some mice. **Who am I?**

_____

3. Living with seven people is a nightmare! I wish my stepmom would let me come home, but apparently her mirror says she isn't the "fairest of them all" anymore so she sent me away. **Who am I?**

_____

4. Some think I'm a criminal, but most people around here call me a hero. I'm great with a bow and arrow, and I never forget to tip! **Who am I?**

_____

5. When I sold our family cow for magic beans, boy did I get in trouble with my mom! I could have never imagined what would happen the morning after I threw the beans out the window. **Who am I?**

_____

6. I'll never visit the swamp again! No more fly lunches for me, thanks. I'm just lucky the princess came around to give me a smooch. **Who am I?**

_____

7. My sister and I got lost in the woods, but we ended up finding a really delicious looking house. Too bad this crazy lady locked us up. Time to find an escape route! **Who am I?**

_____

8. I loved the prince so much that I left my home for him. I even lost my voice in the process! I'm still getting used to the whole walking thing. **Who am I?**

_____

9. I'm a master improviser—I made a ladder out of my hair. This tower sure is high, though. I hope someone comes to save me. **Who am I?**

_____

10. I was so hungry, but now I'm stuffed. Porridge isn't my favorite, but it'll do in a pinch. I'm so sleepy, maybe I'll find a place to nap... **Who am I?**

_____

ANSWERS

The Common Cold

Most people will catch a cold at some point in their lives. Try answering these questions about the common cold. The letter of each answer corresponds to a blank in the secret message at the end of the quiz. Get the answers right to uncover a secret message!

1. Which of the following is a symptom of the common cold?

F. a high fever

G. a runny nose

H. spots on the skin

I. itchy hands

2. What is considered the best way to avoid catching a cold?

R. wearing a mask

S. wearing a hat

T. washing your hands

U. eating lots of fruit

3. What is the cause of the common cold?

M. cold weather

N. stale air

O. a virus

P. lack of sleep

4. What does your body use to fight off a cold?

R. antibiotics

S. vitamins

T. red blood cells

U. white blood cells

5. How many colds does the average child get a year?

T. 1 to 2

U. 3 to 4

V. 4 to 6

W. 5 to 7

6. How long does a cold typically last?

    A. 7 to 10 days   **C.** 1 or 2 days

    B. 2 weeks   **D.** almost a month

7. Who is the only person who can tell for sure if you have a common cold?

    W. a parent   **Y.** a doctor

    X. a friend   **Z.** a teacher

Answers

1. (G)   **3. (O)**   **5. (W)**   **7. (Y)**

2. (T)   **4. (U)**   **6. (A)**

What do you do when a dinosaur sneezes?

___ E ___   ___ ___T OF THE ___ ___ ___!
(1) (2)   (3) (4)   (5) (6) (7)

Answer: GET OUT OF THE WAY!

Are You a Good LISTENER?

Part of being a good friend is being a good listener. How are you when it comes to lending an ear? Take this quiz to find out!

	LIKE ME	NOT LIKE ME
1. If my friend is having a problem, I do my best to help him or her out, even when it's hard.	◯	◯
2. I'm usually the one my friends come to when they need to get something off their chests.	◯	◯
3. I can remember the dates of my friends' upcoming recitals and sports games.	◯	◯
4. When someone is talking, I don't usually interrupt.	◯	◯
5. When someone is telling me a story, I ask questions.	◯	◯
6. I enjoy talking to my friends on the phone.	◯	◯
7. I participate in class and answer questions when called on.	◯	◯
8. If someone gives a presentation, I usually ask them a question at the end.	◯	◯

9. If I need to ask a question about something in class, I wait until I am called on.

○ ○

10. I don't usually have a hard time remembering directions.

○ ○

11. I get excited when people tell me they have big news.

○ ○

12. I don't get bored easily when people are talking.

○ ○

13. I'm a good note-taker in class.

○ ○

14. When doing group work, I'm comfortable recording my group's notes and answers.

○ ○

If you answered mostly "Like Me..."

Congratulations, you are an awesome listener! You pay close attention to what people say, and chances are, people pay you the same respect back. You can be counted on to recall information and to remember the important things in your friends' lives.

If you answered mostly "Not Like Me..."

You may need to work on your listening skills. Whether it's with classwork or friends, sometimes you might let your mind wander, or you might interrupt to let people know your opinion. But it's okay! Next time something requires your attention, make a strong effort to focus. Think about questions you may want to ask when the person is done speaking.

BACK TO SCHOOL

It's time for school! Are you ready for the new year? See if you are by trying your hand at filling in these blanks!

1. My favorite subject is _____ studies because I enjoy learning about history and different societies around the world.

2. Around the middle of the day, students start heading toward the _____ for a well-deserved break!

3. I like using _____ to study for tests. They're small enough to take anywhere and really help with memorizing things.

4. Track, Newspaper, and Film Club are some of the _____ activities I participate in after school.

5. If I need to leave the classroom, my teacher is sure to give me a _____ _____.

6. At the beginning of each year, teachers assign us each different
_____. They can be pretty heavy sometimes!

7. When I'm in math class, I never forget my trusty _____.

8. In gym class we play _____ and I love spiking the
ball over the net!

9. I keep a copy of my _____ close by so I never
forget which class is next.

10. I'm so excited! Our teacher passed out permission slips so we
could all take a _____ _____ to the zoo.

11. In _____ _____, it's very important to clean up
your workstation, and to pay close attention to any safety rules
that your chemistry teacher tells you.

12. Sometimes we read _____ in English class,
and everyone gets to be a different character.

ANSWERS

Welcome Back!

Q: Where in the U.S. can you find a replica of the famous Parthenon in Greece?

A: Nashville, Tennessee

Q: What independent countries make up the island of Hispaniola?

A: The Dominican Republic and Haiti

Q: What country's name, in its people's own language, means "central glorious people's united country"?

A: China

Q: At what height is a hill usually considered to be a mountain?

A: There is no rule or standard about this—it depends on what is nearby. A mountain is a landform that is significantly higher than the surrounding area.

Q: What is the capital of New Zealand?

A: Wellington (It was named in honor of Arthur Wellesley, the first duke of Wellington, who was a hero of Britain's war against Napoleon.)

Q: In which U.S. State would you find Crater Lake?

A: Oregon

Q: Which of these island nations is not in the Indian Ocean: Comoros, Fiji, Maldives, Seychelles?

A: Fiji, which is in the South Pacific Ocean

Q: How many time zones does Alaska have?

A: Two (Before 1983, it had four.)

Q: In 1884, archaeologists began unearthing a great ancient city dominated by a massive structure called the Pyramid of the Sun. The pyramid is 216 feet tall, with a base covering nearly 10 acres. Where is it?

A: The city—called Teotihuacán (tay-oh-tee-wa-kan), City of the Gods—is in Mexico.

Nursery Rhymes

Nursery rhymes have been around for a long time. They are still told to children today. Do any of these classic rhymes ring a bell? See if you can fill in the blanks!

1.

Little Miss Muffet
Sat on a tuffet,
Eating her curds and _____;
Along came a _____,
And sat down beside her,
And frightened Miss Muffet away.

2.

Old Mother Hubbard
Went to the _____
To get her poor dog a _____;
But when she came there
The _____ was bare,
And so the poor _____ had none.

3.

Jack, be nimble,
Jack, be _____;
Jack, jump over
The _____.

4.

Baa, baa, black _____,
Have you any wool?
"Yes sir, yes sir,
Three bags _____.
One for my master,
And one for my dame,
But none for the _____ boy
Who _____ down the lane."

5.

Humpty Dumpty sat on a _____.
Humpty Dumpty had a great fall.
All the king's _____ and all the
king's men
Couldn't put Humpty _____ again.

6.

_____ a song of sixpence,
A pocket full of rye;
Four and twenty _____
Baked in a _____.

When the _____ was opened,
The birds began to sing;
Was not that a dainty _____,
To set before the _____?

ANSWERS

Nature Knowledge

Test your knowledge of nature by reading the questions and taking a guess at the answers!

Q: How long does it take to boil a three-minute egg in Denver, Colorado?

A: Four minutes:
(The higher the altitude, the lower the air pressure—and the longer it takes water to boil.)

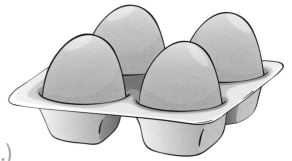

Q: How many sides (or branches) does a snowflake have?

A: Six

Q: How deep is the ocean?

A: 36, 201 feet (at Earth's lowest point, the Mariana Trench in the western North Pacific Ocean)

Q: Is there such a thing as red rain?

A: Yes. Winds blow red dust from the Sahara Desert high into the air. Water vapor condenses around the dust and falls in parts of Europe as red rain.

Q: Which planet in our solar system spins backward?

A: Venus. (Viewed from above its north pole, Venus spins clockwise. The other planets spin counterclockwise.)

Q: The state with the record maximum precipitation in a year is Hawaii. What state has the record minimum precipitation?

A: California. (California had 0.00 inches in 1929. Hawaii had 704.83 inches in 1982.)

Q: Which area is home to more penguins, the North Pole or the South Pole?

A: The South Pole (All penguins live in the Southern Hemisphere. There are none at the North Pole.)

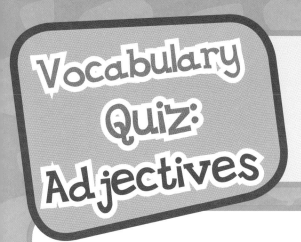
Vocabulary Quiz: Adjectives

Adjectives are words used to describe something. "Lazy" is the adjective in this sentence: The lazy dog slept. Look at the list of adjectives below. Try reading each sentence and placing the correct adjectives in the blanks. If you get stuck, try finding clues in the sentences!

| complicated | stubborn | daring | lighthearted | loyal |
| talented | energetic | protective | consistent | inventive |

1. The firefighters were _____ and saved the kitten from the tree even though there was lightning in the distance—how brave!

2. He is always _____ when turning in his homework; he never misses an assignment.

3. Sandra creates the most breathtaking paintings and we all agree that she is the most _____ student in art class.

4. Even though the assignment seemed simple at first, it was actually _____ and took more time than expected.

5. The school play was _____ because it didn't focus on anything dark, scary, or serious.

6. She is very _____ of her trading card collection and will only let her closest friends touch the cards.

7. The parade float fell apart at the last minute, but we were _____ and came up with a way to fix it fast.

8. A dog is known for being _____ — even if its owner goes away for a while, the dog will remember him or her when they come home!

9. The mule was being very _____ when it refused to pull the wagon full of hay.

10. Ballet dancers need to be _____ enough to leap through the air and dance across the stage many times during one show.

ANSWERS

Are You Too COMPETITIVE?

Being competitive and ambitious is a good thing, unless we take things too seriously. Is your drive to be the best getting in your way? Take this quiz to find out!

	LIKE ME	NOT LIKE ME
1. If my team loses a basketball game in gym class, I'm annoyed for the rest of the day.	◯	◯
2. If someone scores more points on a test than I do, it doesn't matter whether or not I got an A.	◯	◯
3. I only play games if everyone understands all the rules.	◯	◯
4. I'd pick the class star athlete over my best friend when making teams in gym class.	◯	◯
5. It's always good to have a neutral person keep score so that no one can cheat.	◯	◯
6. If I don't make the team, I'll be too embarrassed to try out again next year.	◯	◯
7. Practice doesn't really matter—you're either good at something, or you're not.	◯	◯

8. I've argued with friends over who is best at something.

9. There's no point in doing something if you can't be the best at it.

10. If a teacher lets me know I need to improve in a subject, I get too frustrated to study.

11. If someone picks a topic for a presentation that is too similar to mine, I'll change my topic—even at the last minute.

12. I sometimes get jealous of people who win more awards or get more attention for their skills than I do.

13. I think it's unfair when a teacher holds up someone's work to praise it—it's not like it is better than my work.

If you answered mostly "Like Me..."

Being competitive is one thing, but being mean to others—or mean to yourself—because you want to be the best isn't fair. Not everyone can be good at everything, and that means you, too! Think about how you sometimes act in school or during sports. What do you say or do that might hurt others? Remember, you are talented and special in ways that are all your own. Don't stress if you're not number one all the time!

If you answered mostly "Not Like Me..."

Chances are you handle losing and winning with respect and a clear head. If you ever feel down because you aren't the best at something, just think of all the things you ARE good at. When you don't sweat the small stuff, and bounce back from things that might be disappointing, people see you as an example of a cool, collected person. Good for you!

History Buff

Below is a list of historical events. Try putting the events in the correct order, beginning with the earliest event and ending with the latest event. This one might take some research!

A. Women in the United States gain the right to vote.

B. American colonists sign the Declaration of Independence and the American Revolution begins.

C. Mount St. Helens erupts in Washington.

D. The first computer becomes available at the price of one million dollars.

E. George Washington becomes the first President of the United States.

F. World War II ends.

G. Abraham Lincoln is assassinated.

H. The Berlin Wall comes down.

I. The Tohoku earthquake and tsunami hit Japan.

J. The United States elects its first African-American president.

K. World War I ends.

L. The Wright brothers take their flying machine for a ride.

M. Martin Luther King, Jr. delivers his "I Have a Dream" speech.

N. The United States lands a spacecraft on the moon.

O. The Pilgrims anchor the Mayflower in Plymouth, Massachusetts.

ANSWERS

1. O	**6.** K	**11.** M
2. B	**7.** A	**12.** C
3. E	**8.** F	**13.** H
4. G	**9.** D	**14.** J
5. L	**10.** N	**15.** I

What's Your Style?

Everyone has their own style–what you wear can say a lot about who you are! Take this quiz to determine your own personal style.

Sporty · Classic · Runway

1. You see a new pair of sneakers at the mall. What do you do?
- **A.** Buy them! My old pair is falling apart. (1)
- **B.** I'll get them if I like the color. Sneakers always come in handy. (2)
- **C.** Keep moving–you'll never see me in sneakers! (3)

2. After school you can be found:
- **A.** Polishing an article for the school's newspaper. (2)
- **B.** Practicing my lines for the school play. (3)
- **C.** Running warm-up laps on the track. (1)

3. What's your favorite way to wear your hair?
- **A.** Straightened and sleek, with a sparkly clip on one side. (3)
- **B.** Up in a ponytail and out of the way! (1)
- **C.** Either down or up, but with a little wave to keep things interesting. (2)

4. What's your dream vacation destination?
- **A.** Paris, splitting my time between museums and shopping! (3)
- **B.** Cairo, to see amazing ruins and explore the exotic streets. (2)
- **C.** Grand Canyon National Park. Hiking my way to the bottom would be a blast! (1)

5. Which breed of dog do you like the best?
- **A.** Border collie–they're fast, smart, and always willing to leap for a Frisbee. (1)
- **B.** Golden retriever–they have beautiful coats and aren't afraid to go for a run. (2)
- **C.** Pomeranian–they're small, fluffy, and fit right in a lap! (3)

Sporty 5-8 points

Your style is Sporty. You prefer sneakers to flats, a ponytail to curls, and are most likely a very active person. You keep it simple and fun!

Classic 9-11 points

Your style is Classic. You're not overly flashy, but you like to keep things coordinated. Your outfits are planned down to the smallest accessories, and you love looking and feeling pretty!

Runway 12-15 points

Your style is Runway. You're the trendsetter at your school—you keep up with the latest fashions, and when it comes to hair, makeup, and accessorizing, you can't be beat!

What Scientific Field Suits You?

Do you love science class? There are many different fields of science. Take this quiz to find out which field you're cut out for!

1. **Your room is a mess! You have the whole day set aside to straighten up—what's the plan of attack?**
   - **A.** Organize my stuff into piles before putting it away.
   - **B.** Observe the situation and start working on the areas that need the most help.
   - **C.** Work carefully from one end of the room to the other, making sure everything is in order before moving on.

2. **What kind of books do you like best?**
   - **A.** Anything historical, fiction or non-fiction.
   - **B.** Informative books about animals or the environment.
   - **C.** Science fiction, or books about technology.

3. **You got a few answers wrong on your last math quiz. What do you do?**
   - **A.** Figure out what I'm struggling with and practice the same kinds of questions before the next quiz.
   - **B.** Chalk it up to poor preparation and be sure to study harder next time.
   - **C.** Reread the chapter and see if I can take a retest.

4. **You need to complete a group project and someone cancels at the last minute. How do you feel?**
   - **A.** A little annoyed, but these things happen.
   - **B.** There's always tomorrow!
   - **C.** Stressed, stressed, stressed.

5. **What's your favorite kind of puzzle to solve?**
   - **A.** A choose-your-own-adventure story. Finding clues is the best part.
   - **B.** Something with pictures, like a spot-the-difference.
   - **C.** Sudoku!

Mostly A's

Archeology or Paleontology

You're definitely interested in history, and the idea of life long ago really sparks your interest! In the future, you may just find yourself on an important dig, or exploring some newly discovered ruins!

Mostly B's

Biology or Life Science

All kinds of life are important to you, whether it be animals, plants, or tiny creatures we can't see. You're great at making observations without becoming caught up in getting everything right the first time.

Mostly C's

Chemistry or Physics

Chemistry and physics are all about getting the details – and you're the type to double-check your work! Hard work and a cautious mind are your strengths.

Bears, Bears, Everywhere!

There are different types of bears all over the world. Test your knowledge of these creatures by using the clues to figure out which bear is which. Look at the answer bank below for options!

Polar bear • Grizzly bear • Black bear • Panda • Spectacled bear • Sun bear • Sloth bear

1. I get my name from the light-colored "rings" that appear around my eyes. I live in a warm part of South America, so I don't hibernate like some other bears. Who am I?

_____

2. My coat can range from dark brown to blonde. Sometimes the tips of my fur can be silver or gray, giving me the shaggy look that inspired my name. Who am I?

_____

3. I live in parts of the rainforest—some people confuse me with an extremely slow neighbor of mine. We both have long coats and tend to be lazy! Who am I?

_____

4. I am the largest of the bears, and I'm an excellent hunter. Most bears eat meat and plants, but I stick mainly to meat. **Who am I?**

_____

5. I have an unforgettable face! My markings are special. I eat only ONE thing—a woody plant that grows in China. **Who am I?**

_____

6. Some people say I got my name from the light, round patch on my chest. Others say that it's because I stick to warm climates. I like to build nests in trees and catch some rays! **Who am I?**

_____

7. I am the most common kind of bear in the world. My coat is usually one solid color, except for some lighter fur on my muzzle. I eat anything—animals, berries, roots—even human food! Sometimes it gets me in trouble. **Who am I?**

_____

ANSWERS

Science Fair

Q: What is tetrafluoroethylene resin?

A: The substance better known as Teflon®. A chemist named Roy J. Plunkett discovered it in 1939. Teflon has an unusual property: One side clings fast to another surface (such as a metal cooking pan). Few things, however, will stick to its other side.

Q: What do dynamite and the Nobel Peace Prize have in common?

A: A man named Alfred Bernhard Nobel. Nobel invented dynamite in 1867. Nobel died in 1869. In his will, he left instructions for the establishment of prizes to honor great humanitarian, scientific, and literary achievements.

Q: Whay is syzygy (SIH-zuh-jee)?

A: Syzygy is when three bodies in the solar system—such as Earth, the moon, and the sun—lie in or close to a straight line. This happens twice a month, when the moon is new (its dark side faces Earth) and when it is full (completely lit).

Q: How fast does sound travel?

A: The speed of sound varies, depending on the altitude, temperature, and density of the air it is traveling through. At sea level the speed of sound is about 761 miles per hour.

Q: What is Sedna?

A: A planet–like object orbiting the sun, discovered in 2003. Sedna is the most distant known object in the solar system. Sedna is so far out that it takes 10,500 Earth years for it to orbit the sun.

Q: What does it mean when a weather forecaster says, "It will be partly cloudy"?

A: It means that clouds will block out 35 to 65 percent of the sky. "Mostly clear" or "mostly sunny" means that only 12 to 25 percent is blocked, while "mostly cloudy" is 75 to 90 percent, and "cloudy" is 90 to 100 percent blocked.

Q: Which star in our Milky Way galaxy is closest to Earth?

A: The sun. It is 92,980,000 miles away. Its light, which travels at 186,000 miles per second, takes 8.3 minutes to reach Earth.

People Say the Darndest Things!

An idiom is an outlandish phrase that expresses a certain feeling. Saying, "It's raining cats and dogs!" to describe a heavy rain is an example of an idiom. How many idioms do you know? Try filling in the blanks!

1. Juan was excited to receive an athletic award, but the ceremony was still a week away.

He didn't want to count his _____ before they hatched.

2. Marshall is super-cool under pressure.

You could say he's as cool as a _____!

3. There's still plenty of time to study for the big exam.

Don't make a _____ out of a mole hill!

4. Lucy was down in the _____

after missing her friend's recital.

5. That spelling test was a cinch.

It was a _____ of _____.

6. Dana felt under the _____ and had to visit the school nurse.

7. Chuck was running late for practice but he made it by the skin of his _____.

8. Madison is such a nice person. She'll help someone out at the _____ of a _____.

9. Our teacher was mad as a wet _____ after we disrupted her during class.

10. Tell me about your summer vacation! I'm all _____.

11. Coach Taylor may sound strict, but she's usually pretty easy on us. Her _____ is worse than her _____.

ANSWERS

1. chickens 2. cucumber 3. mountain 4. dumps
5. piece; cake 6. weather 7. teeth 8. drop; hat
9. hen 10. ears 11. bark; bite

What Do You Want to Be When You Grow up?

You may have the right qualities for your dream job and not even know it! Take this quiz to find out what kind of job you might end up with.

	LIKE ME	NOT LIKE ME
1. I am creative.	♡	♡
2. I am a risk taker.	♡	♡
3. My bedroom is usually a disaster.	♡	♡
4. When I was little, I loved to play make-believe.	♡	♡
5. I never throw anything away.	♡	♡
6. English is my favorite subject in school.	♡	♡
7. I'd rather make gifts than buy them.	♡	♡
8. I like to enter the science fair every year.	♡	♡
9. Even my sock drawers are neatly organized.	♡	♡
10. I exercise as often as possible.	♡	♡

11. History is my favorite subject.

12. I win a lot of trophies and certificates.

13. I never miss entering a talent show.

14. I read the newspaper at least once a week.

15. I get along with everybody.

Tally it up!

If you answered "Like Me" to four or more of these questions:
 # 1, 3, 4, 6, 7, 13, read **Careers A** below.

If you answered "Like Me" to four or more of these questions:
#2, 4, 5, 7, 8, 9, 12, read **Careers B** below.

If you answered "Like Me" to four or more of these questions:
#2, 5, 9, 11, 14, 15, read **Careers C** below.

Careers A

You have a true creative side! You are imaginative and innovative, and strongly drawn to the arts. Consider these careers: artist, entertainer, lawyer, musician, psychologist, teacher, and writer.

Careers B

You are destined for a future in business! You're organized, thoughtful, intelligent, and financially savvy. Possible career paths include advertising, business executive, CEO, company owner, finance, human resources, and sales.

Careers C

You are headed for politics! A natural-born leader, your strengths are in people management and problem-solving. Career choices might be business, community fundraising, and politics and government.

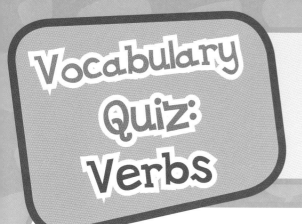

Vocabulary Quiz: Verbs

Verbs are words used to express an action. "Jumps" is the verb in this sentence: Derek jumps over the puddle. Look at the list of verbs below. Try reading each sentence and placing the correct verbs in the blanks. If you get stuck, try finding clues in the sentences!

devour	hike	harvest	avoid	combine
adore	disintegrate	detest	recall	practice

1. The debate team will _____ many times before the big debate next week.

2. Holly likes to _____ a few trails every year and take pictures along the way.

3. Neville can _____ the exact spot where he first rode a bike—he's surprised he can remember.

4. Everyone will _____ Natasha's Halloween costume because she has the best one each year!

5. The whole class _____s book reports, their least favorite type of assignment.

6. If I leave the dog food bag open, Mr. Sprinkles will _____ the whole thing!

7. Each year, California _____s more almonds than any other state in America.

8. If you _____ oil and water, the two substances will refuse to mix.

9. A fish will _____ hunting for food if it is busy guarding a nest of eggs.

10. A heavy rain caused Nolan's notebook to _____—he would still have it if he didn't forget it outside!

ANSWERS

1. practice 2. hike 3. recall 4. adore
5. detest 6. devour 7. harvest
8. combine 9. avoid 10. disintegrate

Animal Trivia

Test your animal knowledge by reading the questions and taking a guess at the answers!

Q: What sea creature rarely gets sick and seems to be immune to all known diseases?

A: The shark

Q: Do polar bears hibernate in winter?

A: No

Q: How many arms does an octopus have?

A: Eight

Q: What type of whale has a spiraled tusk (up to 10 feet long) like a unicorn's?

A: The male narwhal

Q: What type of insect can live the longest?

A: The king and queen termite, which can live 60 to 70 years

Q: Does a painted turtle swallow its food above or below water?

A: Below water (the same as other species of turtle)

Q: What kind of sound does a giraffe make?

A: A low moan

Q: Which U.S. state raises the most turkeys?

A: Minnesota

Q: What color attracts mosquitoes?

A: Blue

It's Just a Fad!

There have been some wacky trends over the years. Test your fad knowledge with this multiple–choice quiz!

1. In the 1970s, people wore these jeans, known for their wide, billowing cuffs.

    A. bell-bottoms   **C.** cutoffs

    B. boot cuts   **D.** camouflage

2. In the early 1990s, kids often played games with small cardboard circles called "pogs." What does "pog" stand for?

    A. People Only Grin   **C.** Passion fruit, Orange, Guava

    B. Play Off Game   **D.** Plenty, Oodles, Glut

3. Drive-in movie theaters were once all the rage. When did the first one open?

    A. 1923   **C.** 1943

    B. 1933   **D.** 1953

4. In 1975, consumers were first able to purchase, name, and take care of pet _____.

    A. tigers   **C.** dandelions

    B. butterflies   **D.** rocks

5. Tie-dye shirts are often associated with the 1960s, but the practice has been going on for a long time. Which country was known to practice the art of tie-dying?

    A. Thailand   **C** Sweden

    B. Nigeria   **D.** Argentina

6. The first coin-operated arcade game was developed in 1966. What kind of game was it?

    A. a submarine simulator   **C.** a tennis game

    B. an alien exploration game   **D.** a puzzle game

7. In the late 1980s, in-line skating, or rollerblading, became popular. What activity did it nearly replace?

    A. skateboarding   **C.** baseball

    B. hop scotch   **D.** rollerskating

8. In the 1920s, women sought greater social freedom. What were young women living during this time nicknamed?

    A. flippers   **C.** floppers

    B. flappers   **D.** fizzles

9. The "beehive" was a tall, round hairdo popular in the 1960s. What was its other name?

    A. the blowout   **C.** the B-52

    B. the balloon   **D.** the bump

Answers

1. (A)   Bell-bottoms were also known as "elephant bells."

2. (C)   The game of pogs originated in Hawaii and was named for a popular Hawaiian juice blend.

3. (B)   Very few drive-in theaters exist today.

4. (D)   The fad didn't last very long, but in the end more than 5 million pet rocks were sold!

5. (B)   Historically, Nigerian women would tie off sections of cloth to dye, creating a splotchy, colorful pattern.

6. (A)   The game cost one quarter to play.

7. (D)   Rollerblades have a single line of wheels, as opposed to rollerskates' pair of wheels by the toe and heel.

8. (B)   The "flapping" came from the sounds women's dresses and necklaces made as they danced.

9. (C)   The haircut was named after the B-52 bomber, a type of plane with a round nose that resembled the hairstyle itself.

Movies, Music, and More

Test your knowledge of movies, music, and more by reading the questions and taking a guess at the answers!

Q: Who was left in charge when the Wizard of Oz left the Emerald City?

A: The Scarecrow

Q: What is the name of Spiderman's true identity?

A: Peter Parker

Q: What are Batman and Robin's real names?

A: Bruce Wayne (Batman) and Dick Grayson (Robin)

Q: Where was the baby Harry Potter and his parents when they were attacked by Lord Voldemort?

A: Godric's Hollow

Q: Popeye the Sailor Man gets his super strength from eating spinach. What food gave his ancestor, Popeye Hercules, super strength?

A: Garlic (He sniffed it.)

Q: Ian Fleming, an author who was a British spy during World War II, created what famous fictional spy?

A: James Bond, agent 007.

Q: The Beatles starred as cartoon characters in what full-length animated film?

A: *Yellow Submarine* (first released in 1968)

Q: What happened to the Three Blind Mice of nursery-rhyme fame?

A: Their tails were cut off by the farmer's wife.

Q: In the Grimm brothers' fairy tale *Hansel and Gretel*, who pushed the witch into the oven?

A: Gretel

Soccer Match

A group of friends is heading off to the big soccer match! Read through the list of events that occur throughout the day. Try putting the events in the correct order, beginning with the earliest event and ending with the latest event.

A. We pick up some snacks and drinks on the way to our seats.

B. We make signs to cheer on our favorite players.

C. Our team scores the first goal!

D. We watch our favorite players warming up on the field!

E. It is 4 to 4 in the shootout and our team is about to kick!

F. A penalty is called at the very start of the second half.

G. The score is still tied at the end of regulation play.

H. We hold our tickets and wait patiently in line.

I. The score is quickly tied up, 1 to 1.

J. We leap from our seats—we won!

K. We figure out where our seats are by looking at the row number on our tickets.

L. The opposing team goes first in the shootout.

M. The team mascot does a dance at halftime.

N. The referee blows a whistle to begin the match.

O. Everyone gets settled in the car—we can barely contain our excitement!

ANSWERS

1. B	**6.** D	**11.** F
2. O	**7.** N	**12.** G
3. H	**8.** C	**13.** L
4. A	**9.** I	**14.** E
5. K	**10.** M	**15.** J

Start Your Engines!

How much do you know about different motor–sports? Try answering the multiple–choice questions below. The letter of each answer corresponds to a blank in the secret message at the end of the quiz. Get the answers right to uncover a secret message!

1. What beverage do the winners of the Indianapolis 500 drink?

    I. milk   **K.** hot cocoa

    J. soda   **L.** orange juice

2. In 1994, what safety feature was added to NASCAR race cars?

    D. roof flaps   **F.** ejection seats

    E. bigger bumpers   **G.** thicker tires

3. What kind of motocross involves riders jumping off ramps and performing tricks for points?

    V. extreme   **X.** free form

    W. competitive   **Y.** freestyle

4. Kart racers ride in low–to–the ground, open cars that resemble go-karts you might see at an amusement park. How fast can the fastest karts go?

    E. over 50 miles per hour   **G.** over 150 miles per hour

    F. over 100 miles per hour   **H.** over 200 miles per hour

5. Hydroplane racing involves extremely fast, lightweight boats. What old-fashioned name is given to its main body?

    D. cockpit   **F.** carriage

    E. canoe   **G.** chassis

6. Many drag races are held by an association called the NHRA. What does it stand for?

P. National High Risk Association

Q. New Hampshire Racing Association

R. No Holds-barred Racing Association

S. National Hot Rod Association

7. What odd vehicle, mostly used for outdoor work, is sometimes raced?

T. lawnmower

U. horse-drawn plow

V. crop duster

W. golf cart

Answers

1. (I) The tradition started in 1936 when winner Victor Louis Meyer asked for a glass of buttermilk. His mother told him to drink it on hot days.

2. (D) The roof flaps help to break up the air flow over a car's roof, and keep it from lifting off the ground at high speeds.

3. (Y) The "Superman seat-grab" is when a rider puts one hand on the handlebars and one on the bike's seat.

4. (G) The fastest karts are called "superkarts."

5. (E) Even though they are relatively lightweight and built for extreme speed, hydroplanes often weight over 6,000 pounds.

6. (S) Some drag racing hot rods can accelerate with the same force as a space shuttle leaving the launch pad!

7. (T) Lawnmower racing was popular enough in 2007 to have its own video game!

What happens to race car drivers when they eat too much?

THEY GET __N__ __-__ __ __ __ION!
(1) (2) (3) (4) (5) (6) (7)

Sports Savvy

Test your sports knowledge by reading the questions and taking a guess at the answers!

Q: Who called dribbling "one of the most spectacular and exciting maneuvers in basketball"?

A: James Naismith, the sport's founder (Dribbling was not part of his original ideas in creating the game. It developed by accident.)

Q: When was the first Kentucky Derby (horse race) run?

A: 1875

Q: In pro sports, who was known as "The Great One"?

A: Wayne Gretzky, professional ice-hockey star.

Q: How many points are scored when an inner bull's-eye is hit during a darts competition?

A: 50

Q: What sport has players who are called "striker" and "sweeper"?

A: Soccer

Q: In what sport are the terms shank, slice, dive, and hook used?

A: Golf

Q: Walter Camp is known as the father of what sport?

A: Football

Q: Which NHL player scored three goals in just 21 seconds?

A: Bill Mosienko, in 1952

Q: A disappointed fan is said to have cried out, "Say it ain't so, Joe!" to a baseball player. Who was that now-famous line for?

A: "Shoeless" Joe Jackson (after the Chicago "Black Sox" scandal of 1919)

Super Structures

How much do you know about the world's most interesting buildings, tourist sites, and other super structures? The letter of each answer corresponds to a blank in the secret message at the end of the quiz. Get the answers right to uncover a secret message!

1. What country boasts an ancient tomb that was designed to allow sunlight to reach a specific spot for only one day a year?

Q. Scotland

R. China

S. Ireland

T. Tunisia

2. How long did the Parthenon in Athens, Greece stand before falling into ruins?

K. over 700 years

L. around 300 years

M. 10 decades

N. 2 centuries

3. What has the Tower of London been historically used for?

P. a palace

Q. a storage tower

R. a clock tower

S. a prison

4. For whom did Shah Jahan build the Taj Mahal?

B. the people of India

C. his wife

D. his parents

E. those visiting India

5. How tall are the highest points of the Great Wall of China?

R. 30 feet

S. 50 feet

T. 100 feet

U. a half mile

6. What is Polynesia's Easter Island famous for?

M. its man-made volcano

N. its impressive fort

O. its homes built from driftwood

P. its massive statues of human-looking heads

7. What can you find at the top of the Empire State Building?

B. a string of decorative lights

C. a bird's nest

D. a glow-in-the-dark sticker

E. a pole from which blimps can be tied

Answers

1. (S) 3. (S) 5. (R) 7. (E)

2. (K) 4. (C) 6. (P)

What is the name given to a super-tall high rise?

__ __ Y __ __ __ A __ __ R

(1) (2)   (3) (4) (5)   (6) (7)

Answer: SKYSCRAPER

The Cat's Meow

Crazy about cats? Test your knowledge of some of our feline friends with this multiple–choice quiz!

1. Some cats are born with multiple _____, a trait they inherit from their parents.

   A. tails   **C.** paws

   B. ears   **D.** tongues

2. Why do cats have small, flexible collar bones?

   A. to help them jump   **C.** to help them climb trees (or furniture)

   B. to allow them to squeeze through small spaces   **D.** to help them land on their feet

3. What do you call a group of lions living together?

   A. a pride   **C.** a gang

   B. a flock   **D.** a horde

4. Cats were highly respected in what ancient society?

   A. Roman   **C.** Aztec

   B. Native American   **D.** Egyptian

5. Why does a cat sometimes bring small animals into the house?

   A. to assert its dominance   **C** to eat in peace

   B. to show its owner some respect   **D.** to claim its territory

6. How many kittens does a cat usually have in one litter?

    A. 1 to 2   **C.** 4 to 5

    B. 2 to 4   **D.** 6 to 8

7. Some people are allergic to cats, but what they are really allergic to is a cat's _____.

    A. saliva   **C.** scent

    B. fur   **D.** meow

8. How old was the world's oldest cat?

    A. 15   **C.** 38

    B. 27   **D.** 51

9. Which of the following is NOT known to make cats sick?

    A. chocolate   **C.** fish

    B. chicken   **D.** cow's milk

Answers

1. (C) The paws on such cats are actually split in the middle, and they can have eight to ten toes on each foot.

2. (B) This feature also allows cats to silently sneak up on prey.

3. (A) Aside from stray house cats, lions are some of the only felines to live in groups.

4. (D) Cats were often mummified and entombed right alongside their masters.

5. (B) Cats view sharing prey as giving a "gift" to the people (or cats) they love!

6. (C) Cats may only have four or five kittens at a time, but a mother cat can have a litter every four months!

7. (A) Cat's groom themselves by licking their fur, and saliva can become airborne this way.

8. (C) Creme Puff was a cat from Texas who died in 2005 at the age of 38.

9. (B) Cats were once fed fish because it was cheap, not because it was good for them!

It's All Greek to Me

The people of ancient Greece had lots of stories to tell! Try answering the multiple–choice questions below. The letter of each answer corresponds to a blank in the secret message at the end of the quiz. Get the answers right to uncover the secret message!

1. The Greek god Zeus gave a woman named Pandora a locked _____, but he told her never to open it. Curiosity eventually got the best of her.

   F. treasure chest   **H.** box

   G. safe   **I.** closet

2. Prince Theseus of Crete was sent to fight the evil Minotaur. The Minotaur was a cross of what two creatures?

   X. human and horse   **Z.** lion and eagle

   Y. human and bull   **A.** lion and goat

3. Icarus and his dad, Daedalus, made wings to fly with. Icarus's wings were melted by the sun's heat. What were they made of?

   R. wax   **T.** feathers

   S. silk   **U.** paper

4. In order to earn his place among the gods, Hercules had to perform twelve tasks, including fighting a monster called the Hydra. What was the Hydra famous for?

   X. its laser vision   **Z.** its powerful venom

   Y. its huge claws   **A.** its nine heads

5. The ancient Greeks believed that souls were taken to a river called the Styx. How did these souls get across the River Styx?

S. a guided boat ride
T. swimming lessons
U. taking a giant leap
V. pole vaulting over the river

6. Medusa was a fearsome creature with snakes instead of hair. What would happen if you looked directly at Medusa?

C. you would run and hide
D. Medusa would disappear
E. you would turn to stone
F. The Hydra would appear

7. Greek legend has it that if you eat something in the underworld, you have to stay there. What did Persephone eat in the underworld to imprison her there?

K. a pomegranate
L. a potato
M. three peaches
N. popcorn

Answers

1. (H)   3. (R)   5. (S)   7. (K)

2. (Y)   4. (A)   6. (E)

What game did kids in ancient Greece like to play?

__ __ **D** __ __ -AND-GO-__**E**__ __
(1) (2)   (3) (4)   (5) (6) (7)

Answer: HYDRA-AND-GO-SEEK

Famous Musicians

Many people have become famous for the music they make. Looking at the clues below, can you name the different musicians? See how much of a music fan you really are! Hint: some of the letters in each musician's name appear below!

1. I'm known as the "King of Rock and Roll" and I was most popular in the 1950s. I once owned a mansion in Tennessee nicknamed Graceland, and people still go there today to learn about me. Some of my most famous songs are about "hound dogs" and "blue suede shoes." **Who am I?**

E_ _ _ _ _ P_ _ _ _ _ _ _ y

2. My nickname is "Satchmo" and I'm most famous for playing the jazz trumpet. I started my career in New Orleans and soon became known for my playing skill and my unusual, gravelly singing voice. One of my best known songs is "What a Wonderful World." **Who am I?**

L_ _ _ s A _ _ st _ _ _ g

3. My nickname is "Old Blue Eyes." I'm known for hanging out with a group of singers called "The Rat Pack." Two of my popular songs are named "Come Fly With Me" and "My Way." I also appeared in several films and performed in places, including Las Vegas, until the end of my career. **Who am I?**

F _ _ _ _ _ S _ _ at _ _

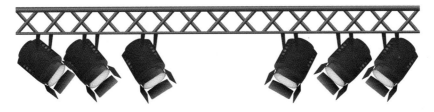

4. I go by one name only, and my nickname is "Madge." *The Guinness Book of World Records* lists me as the best-selling female musician of all time. I've been around since the 1980s, and continue to play huge events like The Superbowl. **Who am I?**

M __ __ __ n __ __

5. Like the lady above me, I go by a single name—and it's my real first name. I started my career in a band called Destiny's Child. I am known for my excellent voice—I can hit a huge range of notes! Sometimes, I also go by the name Sasha Fierce. **Who am I?**

B __ __ o __ __ é

6. I was officially the solo guitarist of the Beatles. **Who am I?**

G __ __ __ __ __   H __ __ __ __ __ __ __

7. I'm famous for my music and my outrageous outfits. I grew up in New York City, and the name I perform under is not my real name. Some of my hits include "Just Dance" and "Edge of Glory." **Who am I?**

L __ __ __   G __ __ a

8. Some of this Australian band's hits were Jive Talkin', Night Fever, and Stayin' Alive. **Who are they?**

The B __ __   G __ __ __

ANSWERS

Scientific-Terrific!

Test your knowledge of science with this multiple-choice quiz. Read each question and see if you can select the correct answer.

1. How long does it take a probe to get to Mars?

A. 7 to 10 months   **C.** 3 to 4 months

B. 30 to 45 days   **D.** one year

2. What does a paleontologist study?

A. bones   **C.** fossils

B. plants   **D.** skeletons

3. Which does the Beaufort scale measure?

A. the density of fog   **C.** the force of waves

B. the speed of wind   **D.** the speed of light

4. Which food squeezed from a tube did U.S. astronaut John Glenn eat in space in 1962?

A. chocolate   **C.** gelatin

B. peanut butter   **D.** applesauce

5. Which is the hottest planet in our solar system?

    A. Mars   **C.** Venus

    B. Earth   **D.** Saturn

6. Which does the U.S. have more of than any other country in the world?

    A. tornadoes   **C.** thunderstorms

    B. hurricanes   **D.** blizzards

7. On average, which ocean is the saltiest?

    A. the Indian Ocean   **C.** the Arctic Ocean

    B. the Pacific Ocean   **D.** the Atlantic Ocean

8. Where does the world's biggest source of energy come from?

    A. solar power   **C.** oil

    B. coal   **D.** generators

Answers

1. (A)	3. (B)	5. (C)	7. (D)
2. (C)	4. (D)	6. (A)	8. (B)

What Does Your Room Say About You?

What if your walls could talk? Well, in a way, they do! Find out what your special space says about you by completing this fun quiz.

Free Spirit · Classic · Laid-Back

1. Which of the following best describes your favorite décor?
- **A.** A mishmash of styles, from wicker and wallpaper to hippie retro
- **B.** Everything color-coordinated, from bed sheets to curtains
- **C.** No real style, just simple and fun

2. What kind of lighting do you prefer for your room?
- **A.** Lava lamps and candles
- **B.** Nice, natural sunlight streaming through your windows
- **C.** Only as much as I need—an overhead light on the ceiling and a reading lamp by the bed

3. What kind of furniture do you like?
- **A.** It doesn't matter—I just paint everything silver, anyway
- **B.** A white canopy bed, with a matching nightstand and dresser
- **C.** The bare essentials—a comfortable bed, a few bookshelves, and a computer desk

4. Where do you do your homework?
- **A.** On the bed or at the dining-room table
- **B.** At the family's old writing desk
- **C.** At the computer desk

5. Which of the following best describes your wall art?
- **A.** Every inch is covered with rock star posters, pictures of friends, and glow-in-the-dark stars
- **B.** Framed photos of friends and family are everywhere
- **C.** A calendar and a bulletin board pretty much mark the spot

Free Spirit

If you picked mostly "A" answers, you're a free spirit! Your room is a fun place, an excellent adventure where a lot is going on. You're a real individual who mixes up your décor and changes it according to how you feel.

Classic

If you picked mostly "B" answers, you're a classic chick! Your dream room is a calm, pleasant place where you can unwind and do your thing in a relaxed atmosphere. Having things match gives you a sense of order in your life.

Laid-Back

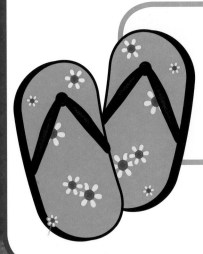

If you picked mostly "C" answers, you're a laid-back lady! You want a space that you can use and enjoy, not take care of all the time. As a result, your room is user-friendly and low-maintenance. You are a cool girl who isn't afraid to express her mellow mood.

Do You Spend Too Much Time with TECHNOLOGY?

Computers, phones, and other nifty devices are great tools for learning and entertainment alike. But sometimes we can get caught up in all this technology! Take this quiz to find out if you need to take a break from the wired world.

	LIKE ME	NOT LIKE ME
1. After school, you can usually find me on the computer.	○	○
2. I usually text when I'm hanging out with friends.	○	○
3. I've gotten in trouble for my cell phone bill.	○	○
4. In class, I've been told to put my phone or music player away.	○	○
5. I'm never without my ear buds, blasting the newest music.	○	○
6. If someone tells me a good joke, I immediately text it to my friends.	○	○
7. I spend three or more hours a day on the computer.	○	○
8. Sometimes, I'll play video games instead of finishing chores.	○	○

	LIKE ME	NOT LIKE ME
9. If I lost my internet connection for a day, I wouldn't know what to do!	◯	◯
10. If I see an ad for a new music player, I want to get it right away.	◯	◯
11. Sometimes I'll argue with family or friends over using the computer.	◯	◯
12. I spend most of my allowance on games for my cell phone.	◯	◯
13. If I need to type a report, I get easily distracted by the internet.	◯	◯
14. I send between fifty and one hundred texts per day.	◯	◯
15. I mostly talk to my friends through text, online chats, or email.	◯	◯

If you answered mostly "Like Me..."

You may be a little too involved in technology. If you're missing out on things—or getting in trouble—because of your enthusiasm for all things tech, it's time to take a step back and rethink your love of technology. Talk to your parents or a trusted adult and ask them to help you get a grip on how much time you spend on your phone, computers, and other devices. Sometimes all it takes is someone to help you take the first step toward a more balanced life!

If you answered mostly "Not Like Me..."

Sure, you like the technology you own. But it doesn't rule your world! You seem to have a good handle on the difference between being tech-savvy and having a tech obsession. Still, you might slip up from time to time. It's hard to keep from getting completely taken in when we're surrounded by neat gadgets! Just remember this golden rule—it's never okay to text or talk on your phone for pleasure when there's company around.

Art History

Below are some questions about the history of art. Take a guess at the answers!

Q: Are most famous artists dedicated and disciplined?

A: Not always. Pablo Picasso frequently skipped art classes in Spain, and Salvador Dali was kicked out of art school! But both dedicated themselves to creating new work, even if they didn't always behave.

Q: Where can you find the world's first works of art?

A: Ancient cave paintings have been found in parts of Europe. The pictures often depict people, as well as the animals that lived alongside these early artists.

Q: How was paint first made?

A: The first paint was probably made by crushing up different minerals or plant matter, and mixing them with water or fat. Today an artist can purchase virtually any color imaginable.

Q: Have art thieves always existed?

A: The first known case of art theft occurred in 1473, when some Dutch paintings were stolen by pirates before being shipped to Italy. Thankfully, the pieces were recovered.

Q: Why do old paintings still look the same after many years?

A: Museums take great care to control the temperature and humidity of gallery spaces and storage areas. This keeps a painting looking its best. People trained in art restoration will also periodically touch up paintings.

Q: Are artists often successful?

A: Sometimes they are, and sometimes they aren't. During his lifetime, Vincent Van Gogh only sold one painting—to his brother. After his death, Van Gogh's work increased in value.

Q: Who was "Mona Lisa"?

A: The subject of this famous painting by Leonardo da Vinci is still a mystery. Still, thousands of people flock to the Louvre in Paris each day to see her.

Addition & Subtraction

1. 10 + 4 + 2 = _____

2. 9 + _____ = 18

3. _____ + 6 + 2 = 8

4. 17 − 6 − 3 = _____

5. 25 - _____ = 19

6. 30 − 13 = 8 + _____

7. Carlos gets 10 dollars for allowance each week. He spends 5 dollars on some candy, and on the walk back from the store, he finds 2 dollars. How much money does he have at the end of his trip? _____

8. Terry's shirt has 11 stripes. Six of them are red, and the rest are green. How many green stripes are on Terry's shirt?

_____

9. Molly is selling apples at the farm stand. She starts with 18. She sells 12, and then a bag of 20 is dropped off. Later, she sells 9 more. How many apples does she still have?

_____

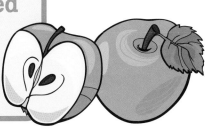

10. There are 2 tigers, 5 tiger cubs, 6 lions, 12 mountain goats, 2 panthers, 1 eagle, and 1 bobcat at the zoo. How many cats are at the zoo? _____

Fashion Through the AGES

Are you a fashionista? How much do you know about the history of fashion? Test your knowledge with this multiple-choice quiz. Read each question and see if you can select the correct answer.

1. Who came up with the idea to add buttons to the sleeves of jackets?

- **A.** Cleopatra
- **B.** Alexander the Great
- **C.** Napoleon Bonaparte
- **D.** Julius Caesar

2. Prior to the 18th century, what did fashion designers use to model their new designs?

- **A.** young children
- **B.** dolls
- **C.** large dummies
- **D.** cardboard frames

3. Queen Elizabeth I of England enacted a law that required all women to wear _____ on Sundays.

- **A.** hats
- **B.** slippers
- **C.** coats
- **D.** belts

4. Heels on shoes have been popular for years. Why were they first added to shoes?

- **A.** to keep the feet away from hot ground
- **B.** to make a person appear taller and more powerful
- **C.** to make it easier to walk uphill
- **D.** to build muscles in the legs

5. What world event saw the creation of the one-piece jumpsuit?

- **A.** The French Revolution
- **B.** the sinking of the Titanic
- **C.** the first Thanksgiving
- **D.** World War II

6. What strange ingredient was used to make early hair dyes?

    A. chocolate   **C.** boiled feathers

    B. crushed tadpoles   **D.** carrots

7. What do the traditional clothing of Rome, Greece, China, India, and Japan all have in common?

    A. they used similar cloth   **C.** they had the same outfits for men and women

    B. they favored pants over dresses and skirts   **D.** clothing was very expensive

8. In early 20th-Century France, what events served as makeshift fashion shows?

    A. masquerade balls   **C.** horse races

    B. harvest festivals   **D.** political speeches

Answers

1. (C)   Napoleon didn't want his soldiers wiping runny noses on their sleeves, so he made them wear buttons to fasten the sleeves.

2. (B)   Small dolls also allowed to save on material costs. Today, real people are used as models.

3. (A)   The law applied to all women and girls older than seven, and violators faced a fine.

4. (A)   Heels originated in the Middle East, where the abundance of sand and sun makes the ground especially hot.

5. (D)   People living in England dealt with air raids, which sometimes required them to jump from bed and dress quickly.

6. (B)   The tadpoles were mixed with oil. Sometimes cow's blood was used, too!

7. (C)   At some point in the Middle Ages, women began wearing dresses. This marked a shift into different clothes for women and men.

8. (C)   Some designers would pay for specific models to attend the races, so that their fashions could be seen by the upper class.

Are You Addicted To Video Games?

Do you spend a little TOO much time in a virtual world? To find out if you're a video game addict, read each statement, then put a check under "True" or "False." When you're done, go to the end of the quiz to see your results!

	TRUE	FALSE
1. I spend more than two hours a day playing video games.	◯	◯
2. The first thing I reach for when I wake up is my video game.	◯	◯
3. My mom often has to pry me away from my video games.	◯	◯
4. I know more about my fave video game than I do about my hometown.	◯	◯
5. I know the release date of every game coming out in the next year.	◯	◯
6. I can rock any video game even with my eyes closed.	◯	◯
7. I have reached the top level of at least ten games.	◯	◯

	TRUE	FALSE
8. I can go days without stepping foot out of my room.	◯	◯
9. My dreams usually involve a video game.	◯	◯

TRUE

If you chose mostly "True" answers, you are addicted to video games, no doubt about it. It's totally cool that you are so passionate about your hobby. But, maybe once in a while, you could step outdoors and see what's going on in the real world, too!

FALSE

If you chose mostly "False" answers, you have your video game habit under control. No need to worry about it! You've done a great job of balancing video games and your social life.

ANIMALS
Down Under

Australia is home to some of the most unusual animals in the world. Find out more about these interesting creatures by taking this quiz.

1. On what important piece of Australian heritage does the kangaroo appear?

- **A.** the national flag
- **B.** the presidential seal
- **C.** the coat of arms
- **D.** the Australian constitution

2. Koalas can eat eucalyptus leaves while other animals cannot because eucalyptus is _____.

- **A.** rare
- **B.** guarded by koalas
- **C.** too high for most animals to reach
- **D.** semi-poisonous to most animals

3. How many pounds will an emu chick gain per week for an entire year?

- **A.** 1
- **B.** 2
- **C.** 3
- **D.** 4

4. Where did dingoes come from?

- **A.** ancient Australian wild dogs
- **B.** the domesticated dogs of Europe
- **C.** they swam from New Zealand
- **D.** no one is sure

5. What does the call of a kookaburra bird sound like?

- **A.** laughter
- **B.** snorting
- **C.** screaming
- **D.** squeaking

6. Aside from being ferocious, Tasmanian devils are also known for what?

A. their intelligence
B. their foul odor
C. their ability to purr
D. their speed

7. What helps a bandicoot feed on tunneling insects and roots?

A. its sharp claws
B. its venom-filled teeth
C. its sharp eyesight
D. its long, thin nose

8. Cassowaries, large, flightless birds, use what feature for protection?

A. their thick feathers
B. their excellent camouflage
C. their helmets, or bony protrusions on their heads
D. their leathery feet

Answers

1. (C) The emu also appears on the Australian coat of arms.

2. (D) Koalas rarely leave trees, so they get their water from the eucalyptus leaf.

3. (B) Emu chicks are born with white stripes on their feathers that fade as they grow.

4. (B) Dingoes look very much like pet dogs, but they are very dangerous and completely wild.

5. (A) Kookaburras are unlike most Australian animals because different varieties of them are found in different parts of the world, like New Guinea.

6. (B) Like skunks, Tasmanian devils produce this unpleasant smell when they feel threatened.

7. (D) Bandicoots hop along like kangaroos, but they are much smaller—usually no more than two feet in length.

8. (C) The Cassowary's helmet protects it from thick jungle plants as it runs through a forest.

I Must Be Mistaken...

Some things are said so many times that we all start to believe the rumors, even if there's evidence to prove us wrong. See if you recognize any of these popular false statements, and try filling in the blanks. Look to the answers for evidence on why you might be mistaken!

1. It is impossible to _____ a piece of _____ more than seven times.

2. The Great _____ of _____ is the only man-made thing you can see from _____.

3. If you eat too much _____, you'll be bouncing off the walls.

4. One ____ in a dog's life is worth _____ human years.

5. Thomas Edison invented the _____.

6. Put on a _____ or you'll catch a _____.

7. Marie Antoinette notoriously said "Let them _____ _____," referring to French peasants.

8. Christopher Columbus discovered that the Earth was _____.

9. Don't read in the _____ or you'll damage your _____.

10. Vikings had sharp, pointed _____ on their _____.

ANSWERS

1. fold; paper. In 2002, a high school student successfully folded a piece of gold leaf more than seven times with tweezers.

2. Wall; China; space. If you are close enough to the Earth to see the Great Wall of China, you are also close enough to see things like highway systems and city lights.

3. sugar. Sugar alone does not cause hyperactivity, nor does it have an affect on gravity. There is no evidence that eating a high-sugar diet will induce hyperactivity. However, it will cause damage to teeth and will likely cause weight gain, so a high-sugar diet is not recommended for anyone.

4. year; seven. Life expectancy varies wildly across different dog breeds. Dogs also have a shorter "childhood" relative to humans.

5. light bulb. Forty years before Edison produced light bulbs, a British astronomer named Warren de la Rue invented the light bulb.

6. jacket or sweater; cold. The weather does not cause a cold—a virus does. Temperature has no affect on a virus.

7. eat; cake. This exact phrase appeared in a book that was published years before Marie Antoinette became queen of France.

8. round. Pythagoras proposed the theory of a round Earth thousands of years before Columbus. Columbus's navigational methods were based on the understanding that the Earth was round.

9. dark; eyes. The human eye is amazingly resilient and reading in dim light will not ruin our eyes. However, reading in dim light does make our eyes work harder and therefore may cause eye fatigue.

10. horns; helmets. There is no evidence that Vikings wore horns on their helmets. It is believed that the first time the image of horns appeared was in an 1876 production of an opera called *Der Ring des Nibelungen*.

Extreme WEATHER

How much do you know abou[t] wild kinds of weather? Find out by marking each state-ment either "True" or "False." Then, check your answers.

TRUE   FALSE

1. A large, powerful storm that can cause tornadoes is called a "superstorm."   ○   ○

2. Large hail can span several inches across.   ○   ○

3. Tsunamis are big storms caused by waves.   ○   ○

4. One of the snowiest cities in North America gets up to 80 inches of snow a year.   ○   ○

5. It only takes two feet of water to cause a car to float away.   ○   ○

6. Doppler radar works together with satellites to detect poor weather conditions before they happen.   ○   ○

	TRUE	FALSE
7. Thunder and lightning are not related.	◯	◯
8. Strong winds have been known to increase the destruction caused by wildfires.	◯	◯
9. Tornadoes are extremely predictable.	◯	◯
10. Hurricanes normally last a week or so.	◯	◯

Answers

1. False. This kind of storm is called a supercell.

2. True.

3. False. Tsunamis are large, destructive waves sometimes caused by earthquakes.

4. False. Rochester, New York can receive over 90 inches of snow in a year.

5. True.

6. True.

7. False. Thunder is the sound lightning makes when it splits the air—sound travels slower than light, so you see the lightning before you hear it as thunder.

8. True.

9. False. Scientists are still unsure why tornadoes start and what makes them stop.

10. True.

Where in the World?

Earth is an amazing place with tons of record-breaking, brain-busting stuff! Take this multiple–choice quiz to discover awesome facts about the world we live in.

1. Where was the world's hottest temperature recorded?

  A. Libya   **C.** Luxembourg

  B. Lebanon   **D.** Lithuania

2. Where is the world's deepest hole?

  A. Antarctica   **C.** Kenya

  B. Russia   **D.** New Zealand

3. What caused the Mississippi River to temporarily flow backward in the early 1800s?

  A. a hurricane   **C.** large boats

  B. a beaver dam   **D.** earthquakes

4. What country is home to the most people on Earth?

  A. India   **C.** China

  B. The United States **D.** Russia

5. Where is the world's tallest active volcano located?

  A. Hawaii   **C.** Chile

  B. The Philippines   **D.** Mexico

6. What is the world's longest river?

A. The Nile River
C. The Mississippi River
B. The Amazon River
D. The Thames River

7. What is the world's largest island?

A. Maui
C. Iceland
B. Madagascar
D. Greenland

8. Where is the world's driest desert located?

A. Africa
C. The United States
B. Antarctica
D. Central Asia

9. What country contains the most lakes?

A. Mexico
C. Algeria
B. Canada
D. Norway

Answers

1. (A) The temperature was recorded in the city of El Aziza, Libya, at 136 degrees Fahrenheit (57 degrees Celsius)!

2. (B) The hole in Russia is nearly eight miles deep and was drilled for research purposes.

3. (D) The same earthquakes also helped form a lake in Tennessee.

4. (C) China has a population of over 1.2 billion!

5. (C) Chile's Tupungato had its last eruption in 1986.

6. (A) Every second, the Nile spits out about 680,000 gallons of water.

7. (D) Although Australia is larger than Greenland, it is classified as a continent as opposed to an island.

8. (B) A desert is classified by its rainfall, not its temperature.

9. (B) Out of all the lakes in the world, more than half are located in Canada!

Science Class

Test your science knowledge by reading the questions and taking a guess at the answers!

Q: Which animal flies highest, the geoduck or the shelduck?

A: That is a trick question! The shelduck is a small member of the duck family. Like other ducks, it can fly. The geoduck, however, is a large member of the clam family. It can weigh up to eight pounds.

Q: When does a snowstorm become a blizzard?

A: When wind speed reaches at least 35 miles per hour, the temperature drops below 20 degrees Fahrenheit, and visibility is less than one-quarter of a mile.

Q: The moon has no atmosphere. Does that make it warmer or colder than the earth?

A: Both. The side facing the sun gets very hot—about 250 degrees Fahrenheit. Without a "blanket" of atmosphere to hold in some of that heat, the temperature on the side facing away from the sun drops to -290 degrees Fahrenheit.

Q: What does it mean when someone calls a tree deciduous (dih-SIH-juh-wus)?

A: Deciduous trees shed all their leaves one season a year, then grow them back another. Maples and oaks are examples of deciduous trees. Evergreen trees, such as pines, have green leaves (needles) year-round.

Q: What is the greenhouse effect?

A: When sunlight passes through Earth's atmosphere and its heat is trapped close to the Earth's surface, raising the temperature.

Q: What is the difference between a nature reserve and a national park?

A: Both are areas that have been set aside for the protection of the animals and/or plants that live there. However, national parks are open to the public, for people to visit and enjoy, while nature reserves are for wildlife only.

Q: What type of flower is the world's smallest?

A: The Lemma, also known as duckweed, and the Wolffia, also known as watermeal (These tiny plants float on the surface of still water. The blossom is smaller than the head of a pin. The entire plant is only 1/16 inch to 1/8 inch across.)

Let's Play!

Some toys are timeless! Test your knowledge of classic toys with this quiz. The letter of each answer corresponds to a blank in the secret message at the end of the quiz. Get the answers right to uncover a secret message!

1. What toy was invented to give disappointed surfers something to do when the waves were wimpy?

Q. snorkel

R. wakeboard

S. skateboard

T. balloon

2. The teddy bear gets its name from what U.S. president?

Q. Abraham Lincoln

R. George Washington

S. Gerald Ford

T. Theodore Roosevelt

3. Where was the game of checkers invented?

T. North America

U. Egypt

V. China

W. Africa

4. What material were pogo sticks first made from?

F. wood

G. aluminum

H. glass

I. tin

5. Which of the following toys is sometimes used on a competitive level?

- **E.** toy soldiers
- **F.** jump rope
- **G.** jacks
- **H.** beach ball

6. Scooters can be toys or transportation! What country manufactures scooters popular in crowded cities around the world?

- **B.** Germany
- **C.** Lithuania
- **D.** South Africa
- **E.** Italy

Answers

1. (S)	3. (U)	5. (F)
2. (T)	4. (F)	6. (E)

Why did the teddy bear put down his fork?

HE WAS __ __ __ __ __ __ D!
(1) (2) (3) (4) (5) (6)

Answer: HE WAS STUFFED!

Do You Have What It Takes To Be A
Master Chef?

1. Do you like trying new things?
- **A.** Sure!
- **B.** It depends.
- **C.** Not really.

2. How is your hand-eye coordination?
- **A.** Great!
- **B.** It's pretty good.
- **C.** So-so...I can be a little clumsy.

3. You have a research paper due tomorrow and you can't find your notes! What do you do?
- **A.** I can handle this! I comb through my books and try to piece the research back together.
- **B.** I panic a little—this will take all night.
- **C.** There goes my grade...

4. Do you consider yourself a creative person?
- **A.** Yes, I have an eye for design and color.
- **B.** I can be; I really enjoy art class.
- **C.** Sort of.

5. How do you handle criticism?
- **A.** I take it in stride.
- **B.** Well, it's always good to learn how to improve something.
- **C.** It can get to me sometimes.

6. Think: How many different kinds of food have you eaten today?
- **A.** 5 to 6
- **B.** 3 to 4
- **C.** 1 to 2

Mostly A's
Master Chef Material

Star chefs need to be cool under pressure, have a handle on the details, and, above all, have an awesome and adventurous sense of taste. You've got what it takes! In the future, you may find yourself creating menus and running a kitchen.

Mostly B's
Growing Gourmet

You're pretty creative and aren't afraid to try new things, including food. Try to step out of your comfort zone a little bit—experiment with flavors you haven't had before. And hone in on your creative spirit with a dose of drawing, or head to the art museum!

Mostly C's
A Cook in the Making

You might not be the most confident or coordinated person, but that doesn't mean the chef world isn't for you! Focus on your strengths. What types of food do you like? Work off basic flavors and try to think of new combinations. In time, you'll be able to develop the skills that a real chef needs.

The MIDDLE AGES

How much do you know about the Middle Ages? Find out by marking each statement either "True" or "False." Then, check your answers.

TRUE   FALSE

1. Castles were always made of stone, never wood.

2. Farming people were independent and didn't rely on protection from a lord or king.

3. Knights wore suits of armor that made walking around difficult.

4. Medieval markets were clean and safe.

5. Jousting involved two riders on horseback charging at each other, each baring a lance.

6. Hands, instead of spoons and forks, were used to eat.

7. A boy began to train for knight-hood once he became a teenager.

○   ○

8. Music was a part of daily medieval life. Minstrels were beloved members of society.

○   ○

9. Toothbrushes were only used by the very rich.

○   ○

10. Bowling was a sport enjoyed by common Medieval folk.

○   ○

Answers

1. False. Castles were made from wood until fire became a common method of attack!

2. False. Farming people, or serfs, needed protection and lived on land owned by a lord or king.

3. True.

4. False. People in the Middle Ages did not understand how germs could make people sick – lots of markets were dirty.

5. True.

6. True.

7. False. Knights in training could be as young as seven.

8. True.

9. False. Even the rich didn't use toothbrushes—spiced water was rubbed on the teeth instead.

10. True.

Read All about It!

Do you like reading? Think you know a lot about classic stories? Test your knowledge with this quiz! The letter of each answer corresponds to a blank in the secret message at the end of the quiz. Get the answers right to uncover a secret message!

1. What character is famous for his purple crayon that reveals a fantastical world?

N. Charlie

O. Harold

P. Ricky

Q. Nathan

2. In Lewis Carroll's Alice in Wonderland, what game does Alice play with the Queen of Hearts?

J. darts

K. rugby

L. cricket

M. croquet

3. What is the shape of the scar on Harry Potter's forehead?

E. a lightning bolt

F. a star

G. a sword

H. a broom

4. Who is friends with The Man in the Yellow Hat?

P. Curious George

Q. Wilbur the pig

R. Little Red Riding Hood

S. Hansel and Gretel

5. Roald Dahl wrote about a boy names James who lived in a giant _____.

    G. pumpkin   **I.** peach

    H. pear   **J.** pineapple

6. What kind of vehicle is described in Chris Van Allsburg's *The Polar Express*?

    F. an airplane   **H.** a bus

    G. a train   **I.** a cruise ship

Answers

      1. (O)   **3. (E)**   **5. (I)**

      2. (M)   **4. (P)**   **6. (G)**

What is the first thing that Charlotte the spider spells in her web in E. B. White's *Charlotte's Web*?

"S___ ___ ___ ___ ___ ___."
      (1) (2) (3) (4) (5) (6)

Answer: "SOME PIG."

Scientifically Speaking

Test your science knowledge by reading the questions and taking a guess at the answers!

1. Which animal's venom acts as a painkiller that is 200 times better at fighting pain than morphine (a drug used in hospitals)?

A. rattlesnake   **C.** centipede

B. poison dart frog   **D.** black widow spider

2. Which was one of the first computer networks and the forerunner of today's Internet?

A. Google   **C.** AOL

B. Yahoo   **D.** Arpanet

3. What are the tiny dots that make up a picture on a TV or computer?

A. pixels   **C.** graphics

B. scans   **D.** particles

4. What did Willis Carrier (1876–1950) invent?

    A. satellite
    C. air-conditioning
    B. television
    D. refrigerator

5. Which is the largest moon in our solar system?

    A. Pluto
    C. Metis
    B. Mercury
    D. Ganymede

6. Which of the following medieval items weighed 45 to 55 pounds?

    A. medieval swords
    C. medieval tapestries
    B. suits of armor
    D. castle doors

Answers

1. (B)	3. (A)	5. (D)
2. (D)	4. (C)	6. (B)

WHAT'S THE BUZZ?

Bees are nature's hard workers! Take this quiz to find out more about these interesting insects.

	TRUE	FALSE
1. All bees are identical to one another.	◯	◯
2. Bees see every color except red.	◯	◯
3. Killer bees have especially harsh venom in their stingers.	◯	◯
4. Bees sip nectar with a long tongue called a proboscis.	◯	◯
5. A queen bee lays a few dozen eggs per day.	◯	◯
6. Bees have two stomachs—one for collecting nectar and one for digesting food.	◯	◯

7. Beekeepers steal honey from bees and harm colonies.

8. Bees build their homes by secreting wax.

9. Bees are a nuisance to humans and aren't important to the environment.

10. Honey goes bad quickly and needs to be kept on ice.

Answers

1. False. A bee colony is made up of a large queen, as well as female workers and male drones. Each has a different job and appearance.

2. True.

3. False. Killer bees are more aggressive than average bees and attack in greater numbers.

4. True.

5. False. A queen typically lays over a thousand eggs each day.

6. True.

7. False. Beekeepers carefully collect the excess honey from a colony, not all the honey.

8. True.

9. False. Without bees, we wouldn't have flowering plants—including fruits and vegetables—to eat.

10. False. Honey is a poor environment for bacteria and therefore keeps fresh for a long time. People have uncovered honey in ancient Egyptian tombs!

Innovative Inventions

Sometimes inventions can change the way we live! Look at the clues below and try to figure out what inventions are describing themselves.

Fireworks • Microscope • Velcro • Jeans • Refrigerator • Paper • Telephone

1. The first electric version of me became available in 1911. I'm a sort of cabinet that compresses gas to make it super cold. Before me, people had to keep ice handy or food would go bad! **What am I?**

_____

2. In Greek, my name means "far sound." I was responsible for better connecting two major cities, New York and Boston, in 1883. My inventor went on to found a large company that sold lots of versions of me all over the globe. **What am I?**

_____

3. I was created over 5,000 years ago in ancient Egypt. I was first made from pressing wet pieces of a plant—called papyrus—together. Over the years, I've gotten smoother and cleaner, but I'm still plant-based. **What am I?**

_____

4. I first showed up around 1590 in an eyeglass maker's shop in the Netherlands. Galileo improved me later on, and named me occhiolino, which is Italian for "little eye." Over the years, I've helped in the discovery of germs and other tiny organisms, and I'm still used today. **What am I?**

---

5. I was created in the American gold rush of the late 1840s. My inventor, a tailor, saw that the gold miners needed sturdy, reliable clothing, so he made me with strong copper rivets. Nowadays, tons of people around the world own me! **What am I?**

---

6. I was created in China around the year 1000. At first, I was used to create signals and messages during battles. Today, I come in a variety of colors and shapes. I'm mostly used in celebrations, and I only come out at night. **What am I?**

---

7. I was inspired by burrs, the seeds of a plant that have tiny, hook-like structures which allow them to stick to things—like clothing. My inventor replicated the seed's design and now I'm used for fastening clothes, shoes, bags, and lots of other things. **What am I?**

ANSWERS

1. Refrigerator 2. Telephone 3. Paper 4. Microscope 5. Jeans 6. Fireworks 7. Velcro

Creepy Crawlies

Q: How many bugs are there on Earth?

A: It's hard to say—many scientists agree that there are millions of insect species that remain undiscovered! What we do know is that only five percent of all the animals on Earth aren't insects. There are over 30,000 individual species of ants alone. That's a ton of bugs!

Q: How many legs does a centipede really have?

A: Even though its name means "one hundred legs" in Latin, centipedes don't have a set number of legs. They can have between 10 and 20 pairs of legs, or they can even have an odd number of legs.

Q: How dangerous are spiders?

A: Luckily, most common varieties of spider are both shy and non-venomous—still, there are venomous spiders out there! The Brazilian wandering spider produces the most potent venom in the spider world.

Q: What do worms do?

A: Worms play an important role in the environment. Their tunnels allow water to reach deep soil and plant roots, and they provide nutrient-rich fertilizer along the way.

Q: Why are slugs and snails slimy?

A: Slugs and snails both use slime like "breadcrumbs"—they are able to retrace their "steps" to find where they last ate some yummy plants. Slug slime is tough stuff to get rid of, so avoid touching slugs!

Q: How do mosquitoes find their food?

A: Female mosquitoes eat blood. They are able to detect prey by sensing carbon dioxide, the gas we exhale. Mosquitoes hunt mainly at night.

Q: How do wasps make their nests?

A: Wasps form their nests in a variety of ways. Some wasps chew up bark from trees and spit the bark out to form the paper-like walls of their nest. Wasps' nests can span a few feet across!

Q: What do flies eat?

A: Flies eat lots of gross things—garbage, spoiled food, and other waste. A house fly can only eat liquids, but it is able to turn some solids into liquids by vomiting on them!

MAKING MOVIES

Are you a cinema nut? Test your knowledge of film–making with this quiz!

TRUE   FALSE

1. The actor originally set to play the Tin Man in *The Wizard of Oz* was forced to quit after the silver paint irritated his skin.

2. The best way to film a move is on location.

3. Actors only get one chance to get a scene right.

4. Movies were made without sound until the 1920s.

5. A cinematographer's job is to operate the camera.

6. Computer animation has made animated movies much easier to produce.

7. Actors are part of a film's crew.

○ ○

8. The oldest movie theater still in operation can be found in Denmark. It opened in 1908.

○ ○

9. 3-D films can be seen by anyone.

○ ○

10. In Japan, moviegoers like to snack on sugared, baked fish.

○ ○

Answers

1. True.

2. False. Some movies are filmed in huge sound stages. Entire towns can be created in these large buildings!

3. False. Sometimes it takes many, many takes to perfect a scene. The director decides when it's right.

4. True.

5. False. Cinematographers are responsible for deciding what the camera will focus on, but they do not actually operate the camera.

6. True.

7. False. Actors are referred to as "the cast," which is separate from the people behind the camera.

8. True.

9. False. Though available to anyone, 3-D films require the viewer to wear specially treated glasses.

10. True.

World Facts

Test your knowledge of the world with this question and answer quiz. Read each question and take a guess at the answer.

Q: How long is the term of a U.S. senator?

A: Six years

Q: On average, which of the world's oceans is the saltiest?

A: The Atlantic Ocean

Q: Who was the first American woman to walk in space?

A: Challenger astronaut Kathryn Sullivan, in October 1984

Q: The world's largest coral reef, the Great Barrier Reef, is located in what country?

A: Australia

Q: The nickname "Old Glory" refers to what?

A: The U.S. flag

Q: Which is the only continent without deserts?

A: Europe

Q: Who was the first known American female soldier?

A: Deborah Sampson (during the American Revolution)

Q: Venezuela is home to the world's highest what?

A: Waterfall (Angel Falls)

Q: About how many Native Americans live in the U.S. today?

A: Two million (About one-third of them live on reservations)

REAL ANIMAL OR MYTHICAL BEAST?

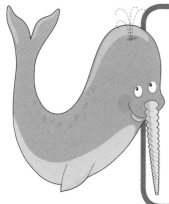

History tell us that people have been making up fantastical creatures for thousands of years. But some real-life animals are so bizarre, it's hard to believe that they exist! Using the clues below, decide which animals are real, and which are made up. Find the answers at the end of the quiz.

REAL ANIMAL

MYTHICAL BEAST

 1. This creature comes in flying and non-flying varieties. It has scaly skin, and its breath is killer. Long ago, some people would find these animals living in caves or old castles, and it'd be their job to get rid of the pesky creatures.

2. This creature moves SO slow, that moss gathers on its fur! It hardly ever touches the ground–in fact, it may live its entire life in trees. Long claws help this creature get a good grip on things.

 3. This desert-dweller hops around with long ears and a cotton tail. It uses its antlers to fight off enemies, and it is known for its ability to run extremely fast.

4. This creature has a beak and can fly. Unlike most birds, though, it has front paws in addition to wings. This creature is so revered that it has been used in architecture throughout history.

5. This creature sports a long horn on its forehead. It prefers cold temperatures, and it loves eating fish. This creature was once hunted to near-extinction.

6. This creature is said to have lived alongside dinosaurs. Though its bite is extremely powerful, a person can easily hold its jaws shut. Historically, people have worshipped this creature, despite how dangerous it can be.

7. This creature has wings but it cannot fly. It has a long, thin beak surrounded by whiskers that work just like a dog's. It is known for the massive size of its eggs.

ANSWERS

1. Mythical beast. Dragons don't exist, but komodo dragons are real, huge lizards that have sharp teeth and bacteria-filled mouths—talk about killer breath!

2. Real animal. There are many types of sloth, and most live in the trees of Central and South America.

3. Mythical beast. The jackalope is supposed to be a cross between a jackrabbit and an antelope. It started as a prank by the early settlers of the American Southwest.

4. Mythical beast. Although the griffin, a creature with the head and wings of an eagle and the body of a lion, is not real, it does appear in countless sculptures from different periods in time.

5. Real animal. Narwhals are a type of whale, and the horn, or tusk, found on their foreheads is actually an elongated tooth.

6. Real animal. Crocodiles are capable of living upwards of eighty years!

7. Real animal. The kiwi, a tiny, flightless bird, is closely related to ostriches and emus.

Test Your Knowledge

Test your trivia knowledge by reading the questions and taking a guess at the answers!

Q: Can you name all eight of Santa's reindeer from the famous poem written by Clement Clarke Moore in 1922?

A: Dasher, Dancer, Prancer, Vixen, Comet, Cupid, Donder, and Blitzen (Rudolph the red-nosed reindeer is from a 1939 poem that later became a popular Christmas song.)

Q: Can you write 1776—the year in which the Declaration of Independence was signed—in Roman numerals?

A: MDCCLXXVI (M=1,000; DCC=700; LXX=70; VI=6)

Q: The igloo, a temporary dwelling used by Inuits of northern Canada and Greenland during the winter hunting season, is made of blocks cut from what?

A: Snow (not ice)

Q: How did Hercules, hero of Greek myths, purify himself after committing a crime?

A: He performed 12 "impossible" feats, known as the Twelve Labors of Hercules.

Q: Which famous New York City landmark has 6,500 windows?

A: The Empire State Building

Q: Do Mexican jumping beans really jump?

A: Yes. Each one has a live, one-quarter-inch caterpillar inside. When the caterpillar moves, the bean "jumps."

Q: About how many stone blocks were used to build Egypt's Great Pyramid?

A: 2.3 million

Let's Make Pizza!

Pizza is a tasty treat loved the world over! It's also easy to make at home, with some help. Try putting the following steps in order from start to finish, and maybe you'll be inspired to make your own pizza creation!

A. Place the pizza in a preheated oven, checking every few minutes. Once the crust is golden brown and the cheese is melted, your pizza is done!

B. Using the tips of your fingers, form a ridge along the edge of the circle of dough. This will be the pizza's crust.

C. Slice your pizza into even, triangular slices and enjoy!

D. Sprinkle the pre—made dough with flour and form into a ball.

E. Place the dough ball on a flat, floured surface. Using either your hands or a rolling pin, flatten the dough into an even circle.

F. Carefully slice any toppings—like vegetables or meat—and place them on top of the cheese.

G. Ask an adult for permission and help to start making your pizza.

H. Allow the pizza to cool after removing it from the oven.

I. Sprinkle shredded cheese evenly over the layer of tomato sauce.

J. Use a spoon to place a pool of sauce in the center of the circle. Spread out evenly to the edges, leaving the crust without sauce.

ANSWERS

1.	G	**6.**	I
2.	D	**7.**	F
3.	E	**8.**	A
4.	B	**9.**	H
5.	J	**10.**	C

Fun on the FARM

Farms are fascinating places and they are important to the world—after all, they provide almost all the food we eat. Test your knowledge about farms with this quiz.

TRUE   FALSE

1. Massachusetts produces the most cranberries in America.

2. A single cow can produce 46,000 glasses of milk in a year.

3. More than half the amount of tomatoes Americans eat in a year come in the form of ketchup and tomato sauce.

4. A young female turkey is called a Jessica, and a young male is called a Joey.

5. There are only a few varieties of chickens, and they are based on feather color.

6. Crops are rotated to new fields once they are harvested, so the soil has time to recover nutrients.

	TRUE	FALSE

7. Some soaps are made from goat's milk.

8. Corn is only eaten on the cob, from cans, as popcorn, or in the form of creamed corn.

9. Some livestock owners will grow crops just to feed their animals, and will sell leftovers as "cash crops."

10. Wheat for pasta must come from a specific variety of wheat called "durham."

Answers

1. False. Each year, Wisconsin produces about 300 million pounds of cranberries.

2. True.

3. True.

4. False. A young female is a Jenny, and a young male is a Jake. Older males are called Toms.

5. False. Chickens come in all sizes and colors, with over 175 different varieties.

6. True.

7. True.

8. False. Corn, and products made from corn, may appear in thousands of items found in your local grocery store.

9. True.

10. True.

Multiplication & Division

Test out your multiplication and division skills! Fill in the blanks to answer each question.

1. $10 \times 3 =$ _____

2. $8 \times$ _____ $= 24$

3. $36 = 6 \times$ _____

4. $12 \div 6 =$ _____

5. $40 \div$ _____ $= 10$

6. _____ $\div 3 = 3$

7. Matt has 7 green marbles and twice as many red marbles. How many marbles does he have in total? _____

8. Tricia had 22 trading cards and gave half away to charity. If she buys 5 more trading cards, how many cards does she end up with? _____

9. Ms. Arnold brought 28 cookies for her students. Half of them were chocolate chip, and the other half were split between sugar and oatmeal raisin. How many oatmeal raisin cookies did she bring? _____

10. Louis spots 6 pigeons on the field. Three times as many pigeons land. Then, half the number of all the pigeons fly away. How many pigeons does Louis see now?

_____

ANSWERS

1. 30 **2.** 3 **3.** 6 **4.** 2 **5.** 4
6. 9 **7.** 21 **8.** 16 **9.** 7 **10.** 12

Nature Fun

Q: If all the water in Earth's atmosphere fell as rain at the same time, about how deep would it be worldwide?

A: Close to one inch (0.98 inch)

Q: Diamond is the hardest mineral. What is the second hardest?

A: Corundum, which is the mineral name for ruby and sapphire.

Q: Is it the youngest or oldest mountains that are the roundest and lowest?

A: The oldest

Q: What type of rock can float in water?

A: Pumice

Q: If all the dry land on Earth was divided equally, about how much would each person get?

A: Six acres

Q: Which provides more heat when burned: a pound of wood or a pound of coal?

A: A pound of coal

Q: Which planet in our solar system has a huge revolving storm known as the Great Red Spot?

A: Jupiter

Q: What was the most rain ever to fall n a 24-hour period?

A: 73.5 inches, on March 15–16, 1952, at Chilaos, Réunion, an island in the Indian Ocean

Let's Watch

Are you a television buff? Do you spend hours watching your favorite TV shows? Test your knowledge of television history with this quiz. Read each question and answer True or False.

TRUE   FALSE

1. Theodore Roosevelt was the first President of the United States to appear on live television.

2. Though color TV was experimented with in the 1920s, the first color TV appeared in stores in 1953.

3. The word "television" comes from the Greek word for "lazy."

4. Twin antennae once appeared on top of televisions and were nick-named "rabbit ears."

5. Some people place small dishes on their roofs to receive signals from sat-ellites that transmit television signals.

6. People from eight to eighteen years old spend an average of two hours a day watching television.

7. Remote controls didn't become available until the 1980s.

○   ○

8. The most watched TV programs are usually news stories and specials.

○   ○

9. The "LCD" in LCD screens stands for Lifelike Cartoons and Dramas.

○   ○

10. You can now find televisions on the back of airplane seats.

○   ○

Answers

1. False. His cousin, Franklin Delano Roosevelt, was the first. He spoke after the 1939 World's Fair.

2. True.

3. False. "Tele" means "far" in Greek, and "vision" means "sight" in Latin. So, television means "far sight."

4. True.

5. True.

6. False. People in this age group typically watch four or more hours of television daily.

7. True.

8. False. Global sporting events, like World Cup Soccer (Football) and the Olympics, receive the most viewers worldwide.

9. False. LCD stands for Liquid Crystal Display.

10. True.

Worldwide Trivia

Test your worldly knowledge with this multiple-choice quiz! Read each question and see if you can select the correct answer.

1. What is the name of the 19.5-foot statue on top of the Capitol Building in Washington, D.C.?

    A. Capitol   **C.** Freedom

    B. Patriot   **D.** Liberty

2. In what country would you find the Taj Mahal, a famous mausoleum?

    A. Egypt   **C.** Brazil

    B. India   **D.** Ghana

3. Where did Theodore Roosevelt travel when he became the first president in office to travel outside of the U.S.?

    A. Italy   **C.** Cuba

    B. Panama   **D.** England

4. How tall is the Eiffel Tower?

    A. 1,063 feet   **C.** 500 feet

    B. 2,336 feet   **D.** 3,145 feet

5. Which of the following presidents has the most places named after him?

A. Theodore Roosevelt   **C.** Abraham Lincoln

B. John F. Kennedy   **D.** George Washington

6. Famous Spanish painter Pablo Picasso is the founder of which style of painting?

A. Expressionism   **C.** Cubism

B. Surrealism   **D.** Impressionism

7. Russia is the largest country in the world. What country is the second largest?

A. China   **C.** United States

B. Canada   **D.** Brazil

4. What was the primary purpose of the famous Roman Coliseum?

A. entertainment   **C.** education

B. punishment   **D.** trade

Answers

1. (C)	3. (B)	5. (D)	7. (B)
2. (B)	4. (A)	6. (C)	8. (A)

What's Your Olympic Event?

Ever dream of competing at the highest level of sport, the Olympic games? Take this quiz to figure out what event you might be able to master!

1. It's time to take a vacation! You can go anywhere you'd like, and do anything you'd like—what's the plan?
- **A.** Camping, with some hiking and fishing mixed in.
- **B.** Definitely the beach, with lots of friends.
- **C.** Somewhere with plenty of museums.

2. What is your ideal summer job?
- **A.** Neighborhood dog walker—all the exercise will be great!
- **B.** Something at the local ice cream place. It's nice to be around people all day.
- **C.** Camp counselor. I can help others learn some of the activities I love!

3. You want to throw your best friend a birthday party. What do you do?
- **A.** Spend the whole day running errands—getting a cake, balloons, decorations, the works!
- **B.** Gather up your group of friends and brainstorm some fun party ideas.
- **C.** Write up an invitation and pick a restaurant you know your friend will love.

4. Where do you like to study?
- **A.** In the park or at a cafe.
- **B.** At the library with a study group.
- **C.** In my room or curled up on the couch.

5. Cats or dogs?
- **A.** Dogs, definitely!
- **B.** I really don't mind either one.
- **C.** Cats are more my style.

Mostly A's
Track and Field

You're the kind of person who likes to be active constantly – the perfect sort of energy needed to be a track star! Keep your eyes on the prize and push yourself to reach your goals on and off the field.

Mostly B's
Team Sports Like Soccer, Volleyball, or Basketball

Working in groups is where you do your best. Quick thinking and an ability to work well with others make you the perfect team player.

Mostly C's
Individual Sports Like Archery, Fencing, or Singles Tennis

You work best under pressure, especially when the pressure is all on you. Individual sports require a ton of concentration and discipline. You've got what it takes!

Birds of a Feather

Birds are found all over the world, and each kind is different. Try out your knowledge of feathery friends with this quiz. The letter of each answer corresponds to a blank in the secret message at the end of the quiz. Get the answers right to uncover a secret message!

1. Not all owls live in trees. Where do many owls in North and South America make their nests?

O. in water

Q. underground

P. in caves

R. in people's homes

2. What is the fastest, largest bird that also lays the biggest eggs?

U. ostrich

W. albatross

V. emu

X. dodo

3. What were homing pigeons once used for?

X. food

Z. pest control

Y. locating other birds

A. carrying messages

4. What is the most common kind of bird in the world?

B. sparrow

D. pigeon

C. chicken

E. crow

5. What physical feature allows birds to fly?

j. tiny feet

L. feathers

K. hollow bones

M. strong muscles

6. What bird is able to fly backward?

    C. peacock   **E.** hummingbird

    D. turkey   **F.** cardinal

7. Why do some male birds have bright, colorful feathers?

    O. to help them blend   **Q.** to scare away enemies
        in with flowers   **R.** to attract a mate

    P. to attract insects

8. What do we call the group of meat-eating birds with sharp beaks and talons?

    R. eagles   **T.** hawks

    S. raptors   **U.** hunters

Answers

1. (Q)	3. (A)	5. (K)	7. (R)
2. (U)	4. (C)	6. (E)	8. (S)

What does a duck like to eat with soup?

___ ___ ___ ___ ___ ___ ___ ___
(1) (2) (3) (4) (5) (6) (7) (8)

Way Back When

Test your history knowledge by reading the questions and taking a guess at the answers!

Q: How many expeditions did Christopher Columbus make to the new world?

A: Four

Q: What was a popular male fashion trend in ancient Greece?

A: Wearing a beard, real or fake

Q: Where did the tradition of giving Easter eggs to children come from?

A: In ancient Persia (now Iran), it was traditional to give eggs to friends in the springtime.

Q: Who made this famous statement: "I only regret that I have but one life to lose for my country"?

A: Nathan Hale, a schoolteacher who joined the American army during the American Revolution. He said this statement before being hanged as a spy.

Q: Where and when were the first hard candies made?

A: Egypt, around 1000 B.C.

Q: At one point in history, why did people in Scotland refuse to eat potatoes?

A: They were not mentioned in the Bible.

Q: Where did the coffee plant originate?

A: Ethiopia

Q: What was an early 18th century form of bicycle called?

A: "Dandy horse"

Q: According to legend, who were Romulus and Remus?

A: Twins who founded the city of Rome

Animal Kingdom

Can you identify lots of different animals? Flex your skill by reading these clues and figuring out which animal is which!

Anaconda • Anglerfish • Chimpanzee • Hippopotamus • Meerkat • Parrot • Peregrine falcon • Polar bear • Siberian tiger • Wild mustang

1. My tusks and short temper make me the most dangerous animal in Africa, more dangerous than lions. I love water so much that my name means "water horse" in Greek. **Who am I?**

_____

2. I catch my prey by dangling a long appendage in front of my face. You could say that I love fishing so much, it's part of my name. I live in a deep, dark place where no one can go. **Who am I?**

_____

3. I am the fastest animal on Earth. I have special flaps over my nose to keep fast-moving air out as I fly through the sky. I have been clocked at speeds close to 200 miles per hour. **Who am I?**

_____

4. I live and hunt in a very cold place. Though I may look white, my fur is actually clear and reflects the environment around me. I have cousins all over the world. **Who am I?**

_____

5. Even though I eat with my feet, I have the intelligence of a six-year-old human. Some people say I can talk! Most of us are brightly colored. **Who am I?**

_____

6. I am larger than my close cousin in India, and I like colder weather, too. I am very endangered, and my territory sometimes overlaps with grizzly bear territory. **Who am I?**

_____

7. I am the largest of my kind on Earth. I love hanging out in the wet Amazon rain forest, and I only become active every few months to squeeze some prey. **Who am I?**

_____

8. My large family lives on the African plains, and we build nests in tunnels and holes. I spend a lot of my time standing on my back legs, checking for danger. **Who am I?**

_____

9. My family and I roam the plains of the American west and southwest. Even though I roam wild, I was once owned by the people who first settled America. I love to run! **Who am I?**

_____

10. I am the closest relative of humans. I appear in movies and in TV, but my real home is in Africa. I don't have a tail, but I have thumbs for eating lots of plants and fruit. **Who am I?**

_____

ANSWERS

1. Hippopotamus 2. Anglerfish 3. Peregrine falcon 4. Polar bear 5. Parrot 6. Siberian tiger 7. Anaconda 8. Meerkat 9. Wild mustang 10. Chimpanzee

SCIENCE FICTION... OR SCIENCE FACT?

Science fiction often tells us about products or events that are too cool to be true. But, sometimes, things that may sound like sci-fi are amazing AND real! Read each description below and decide what is science FICTION and what is science FACT!

SCIENCE FICTION

SCIENCE FACT

1. Scientists have developed a type of wheel-less bike that can hover inches off the ground.

2. Spectators at a high school football game in Arizona witnessed several UFOs—unidentified flying objects—in the nighttime sky.

3. In 1938, radio listeners were warned of a Martian attack and were evacuated from cities to avoid the coming invasion.

4. Scientists have developed robots that can perform complicated medical procedures like open-heart surgeries and organ transplants.

5. Over the centuries, dogs have adapted to learn our language and they use it to communicate with us.

6. Spacecraft can enter into "hyperspace," in which a ship travels faster than the speed of light.

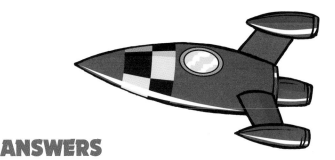

ANSWERS

1. Science fact. This hover bike is large and doesn't move very fast, but a California-based company plans to market it to everyday people in the near future. Imagine riding to school in that!

2. Science fiction. The "UFOs" turned out to be late night sky divers holding road flares.

3. Science fiction. While listeners did receive a warning, there was no invasion—the broadcast was a prank played by radio personality Orson Welles. It caused people to panic, and Welles got in serious trouble for causing such an uproar.

4. Science fact. While doctors assist these robots remotely, scientists plan to build more sophisticated robots that will eliminate doctor involvement little by little.

5. Science fact. While dogs can't really "talk," scientists believe that after thousands of years spent in human civilization, they have adapted to understand the different tones we use—like when we're angry, sad, or happy. Think about that next time your dog whines for some of your food!

6. Science fiction. The moon, Earth's closest neighbor, still takes three days to be reached by the fastest, most advanced spacecraft.

THE WILD, WILD WEST

	TRUE	FALSE
1. Cowboys and cowgirls made elaborate, delicious meals.	◯	◯
2. Sawdust covered saloon floors to make the collection of gold dust—brought in from miners—easier.	◯	◯
3. Cowgirls stayed on the farm or in camp.	◯	◯
4. Cowboys and cowgirls would drive cattle for hundreds of miles at a time.	◯	◯
5. A "ten gallon hat" got its name from cowgirls and cowboys allowing their horses to drink from upturned hats.	◯	◯
6. Towns in the Wild West had no laws.	◯	◯

7. Cowboys and cowgirls were known to make up songs while on the trail.

○ ○

8. Rodeos, as we know them today, evolved from cattle roping in the days of the Wild West.

○ ○

9. Theft in the Wild West was not a serious crime.

○ ○

10. Cowboys and cowgirls were also called "cowhands" and "buckaroos."

○ ○

Answers

1. False. Cowboys and cowgirls would often eat in a hurry and store food in easily accessible tins—the food was often not heated.

2. True.

3. False. The famous Calamity Jane was known to fight alongside cavalry missions.

4. True.

5. True.

6. False. As the American West became settled, towns such as Deadwood, North Dakota, developed sophisticated laws and police forces.

7. True.

8. True.

9. False. Stealing—especially stealing horses—was very serious, as people had few possessions and no way to get around without horses.

10. True.

The Amazing Human Body

Test your knowledge of the human body by reading the questions and taking a guess at the answers!

Q: Many people have a malady called furfur. What is it?

A: Dandruff

Q: Where did the expression "goose pimples" come from?

A: From how a goose's skin looks when its feathers are plucked (also called goose bumps or gooseflesh)

Q: What happens to the skin of someone with a disease called ichthyosis (ik-thee-OH-sis)?

A: It becomes dry and scaly.

Q: About how many times does the average human take a breath during a 24-hour period?

A: 24,000

Q: Was the brain of a Neanderthal larger or smaller than ours?

A: Larger

Q: How long does it take for blood to make a complete circuit of the human body?

A: Under a minute

Q: About how long is the small intestine in an adult human?

A: 22 to 25 feet long

Q: If you lose the sight in one eye, how much of your vision do you lose?

A: About one–fifth (but all of your depth perception)

Q: How many miles of blood vessels, on average, are in the human body?

A: About 100,000 miles for an adult; about 60,000 miles for a child

Do You Need Motivation?

Our sense of motivation is what drives us to achieve our dreams and goals. How's your motivation level looking? Take this quiz to find out!

1. **Your art teacher assigns a huge self-portrait project—it's worth almost half your grade for the semester! How do you go about getting this done?**
   - **A.** I work on it a little bit each night until the due date.
   - **B.** I set aside a chunk of time on the weekend to complete it—better to get it done all at once.
   - **C.** I wait until a few days before it's due...I work best under pressure, I think...

2. **Your article for the school newspaper didn't make it into the latest issue. What do you do?**
   - **A.** Go over it again, make some changes, and re-submit it for next month's issue.
   - **B.** Put it away for a while. Maybe I'll see it in a different light later on.
   - **C.** Consider taking up drama club or the track team.

3. **A friend has asked you to participate in a charity bowling event, but bowling is really not your thing. How do you handle this?**
   - **A.** Go, of course! It's for a good cause and I don't want to let my friend down.
   - **B.** I'll go but I might leave early—bowling is SO boring.
   - **C.** Maybe I can just donate some money instead of bowling?

4. **You have a week off from school, but it rains the WHOLE time! How does your week go?**
   - **A.** I straighten up my room and catch up on some books I've been wanting to read.
   - **B.** I relax a lot and spend time with my friends.
   - **C.** I lounge around the house and sulk about the bad weather.

5. Your volleyball coach tells you that you need to work on your serve. How do you react?

A. I ask her if I can get some time in the gym to practice.

B. I worry a little bit, but I know my serve will get better with time.

C. I try to avoid serving whenever possible.

Mostly A's
High Motivation

Wow, you are a true go-getter! You are confident and aren't afraid to take on any challenge. Just remember that sometimes it's okay to take a break.

Mostly B's
Decent Motivation

You've got what it takes to get things done. Sometimes you may doubt yourself, but in the end you achieve the goals you've set for yourself. Focus a little bit more on taking action.

Mostly C's
Low Motivation

Don't be so hard on yourself! The tools to being successful are right in your hands. Try making a clear list of goals, and when you receive criticism, try not to take it so hard. Believe in yourself!

Lights, Camera, Sequence!

It's time to head to the theater! Read the list of events and try putting them in the correct order.

A. We stand in line and wait to buy tickets.

B. We settle down—the previews are starting!

C. The movie is in full swing and action packed—we are on the edge of our seats!

D. We look up what movies are playing.

E. All we can talk about on the ride home is how awesome the movie was!

F. We find the perfect seats.

G. We decide to get some snacks—time to get in line!

H. The final credits start to roll.

I. We whisper about what upcoming movies look good.

J. We head to the theater, leaving early enough to grab tickets.

K. We gather up our trash and exit the theater.

L. We decide on a time to go to the movies.

M. The title screen appears!

N. We hand the usher our tickets.

ANSWERS

1.	D	**6.**	N	**11.**	C
2.	L	**7.**	F	**12.**	H
3.	J	**8.**	B	**13.**	K
4.	A	**9.**	I	**14.**	E
5.	G	**10.**	M		

Are You Cut Out for Camping?

Camping seems like so much fun! Are you cut out for this kind of outdoor adventure? To find out, read each statement, then put a check under "True" or "False." When you're done, go to the end of the quiz to see your results!

	TRUE	FALSE
1. If I could, I would be outdoors all day long.	◯	◯
2. I can build a fire.	◯	◯
3. Insects don't bother me.	◯	◯
4. I don't need a comfy bed to sleep well.	◯	◯
5. I can go days without showering.	◯	◯
6. I don't need gourmet meals.	◯	◯
7. Extreme temperatures don't affect me.	◯	◯

	TRUE	FALSE
8. I have a good sense of direction.	◯	◯
9. I don't need to watch TV.	◯	◯
10. I know the difference between poison ivy and poison oak.	◯	◯
11. I know how to find the North Star.	◯	◯

EXPERT CAMPER

If you chose mostly "True" answers, you are a camper at heart. Sleeping in a tent, even if it's raining, wouldn't faze you in the least. You have what it takes to be an expert camper!

CAMPING ROOKIE

If you chose mostly "False" answers, you might want to rethink that camping trip. You like creature comforts, and camping means roughing it. But give it a try, anyway—you never know!.

Back in Time

Test your history knowledge by reading the questions and taking a guess at the answers!

Q: Why were the mummies of pharaohs (kings of ancient Egypt) often buried in boats?

A: The people of ancient Egypt believed that the boats would carry the pharaohs into the afterlife.

Q: How fast did the original Wright brothers' plane fly?

A: 30 miles per hour

Q: Surgeons in the 17th century performed bloodletting and tooth extraction. What other service did they offer?

A: They gave haircuts.

Q: How long did it take Sir Francis Drake to sail around the world?

A: 34 months (December 1577 to September 1580)

Q: What device did Christopher Columbus use on his voyages to measure the passage of time?

A: A sandglass (also called an hourglass)

Q: George IV, king of England from 1820 to 1830, ordered a pair of boots to fit each of his feet. What was unusual about that?

A: Before then, each shoe was designed to be interchangeable, fitting both the right and left foot.

Q: Before the United Nations moved to its permanent home in New York City in 1951–1952, where was its headquarters?

A: Lake Success, New York

Q: In what country did the windmill originate, in about A.D. 644?

A: Persia (now Iran)

Around The World

Do you know a little about a lot of things relating to our world? Test your knowledge of world trivia with this quiz. Read each question and see if you can select the correct answer.

1. What causes Earth's weight to increase by about 90 tons per day?

    A. dust from outer space   **C.** water

    B. volcano lava   **D.** humans

2. Which of these groups of people live in Antarctica?

    A. whalers   **C.** scientists

    B. eskimos   **D.** fishermen

3. Which state has the largest proven crude-oil reserves?

    A. Louisiana   **C.** Texas

    B. California   **D.** Alaska

4. In 1620, how many days did it take the Mayflower to sail from England to America?

    A. 44   **C.** 22

    B. 90   **D.** 66

5. When was the first Wimbledon tennis tournament held?

  A. 1952   **C.** 1877
  B. 1940   **D.** 1920

6. Which world record does New York City hold?

  A. largest population of people   **C.** most taxi cabs
  B. Most skyscrapers   **D.** oldest church

7. Where is the world's longest road tunnel located?

  A. United States   **C.** Switzerland
  B. Germany   **D.** Australia

Answers

| 1. (A) | 3. (C) | 5. (C) | 7. (A) |
| 2. (C) | 4. (D) | 6. (B) | |

Who Is This?

Test your knowledge of famous American people by reading the questions and taking a guess at the answers!

Q: Who, in 1896, told newspaper reporters this now-famous statement: "The report of my death has been greatly exaggerated."?

A: Mark Twain, the famous author, responding to rumors that he had died.

Q: Jane Goodall is famous for studying what kind of animals?

A: Chimpanzees

Q: The captain of the British ship Endeavour successfully navigated the Great Barrier Reef off the coast of Australia—one of the world's most challenging sea courses. What was his name?

A: James Cook (1728–1779)

Q: Helen Keller could not see, hear, or speak. What was the name of the teacher who helped her overcome her disabilities?

A: Anne Sullivan

Q: Who said, "Genius is one percent inspiration, ninety-nine percent perspiration"?

A: Thomas Alva Edison, the famous inventor

Q: Who wrote, "In spite of everything, I still believe that people are good at heart"?

A: Anne Frank (in *The Diary of Anne Frank*)

Q: Who said, "No one can make you feel inferior without your consent"?

A: Eleanor Roosevelt

Q: What did Charles Dickens, Thomas Alva Edison, and Mark Twain have in common?

A: None of them finished elementary school.

What Animal Are You Most Like?

There are all sorts of personalities, and some people's traits can be compared to those of animals. Take this quiz to find out what kind of animal you're like.

Tiger   Golden Retriever   Turtle

1. You argue with your dad. You:
- **A.** Get upset and throw stuff.
- **B.** Sulk for a while, then talk it out.
- **C.** Hide for a while, then never bring it up again.

2. Your sport of choice is:
- **A.** Wrestling
- **B.** Baseball
- **C.** Golf

3. Your favorite music is:
- **A.** Heavy metal
- **B.** Top 40
- **C.** Jazz

4. Your friends:
- **A.** Are sort of scared of me
- **B.** Love hanging out with me
- **C.** I don't have many friends

5. Your favorite color is:
- **A.** Black
- **B.** Blue
- **C.** White

6. In school, your favorite subject is:
- **A.** Math
- **B.** Gym
- **C.** Science

Tiger — Mostly A's

You are most like a tiger. You can be ferocious and tend to pounce on unsuspecting victims. Keep your fierceness, but tone it down a bit.

Golden Retriever — Mostly B's

You are most like a golden retriever. You are loyal and loved and enjoy hanging out with your friends and doing guy stuff.

Turtle — Mostly C's

You are most like a turtle. You are solitary and keep to yourself. It's okay to come out of your shell once in while!

Icy Cold Fun

Do you enjoy snowy, cold weather or do you prefer warm, tropical weather? Regardless of your preference for cold or warm, you can test your knowledge of icy cold fun facts with this quiz.

1. **In which city was the first artificial ice-hockey rink built in North America?**

    A. New York, New York

    B. Montreal, Canada

    C. Boston, Massachusetts

    D. Seattle, Washington

2. **The greatest single snowstorm ever happened in Mt. Shasta Ski Bowl, California in 1959. How much snow fell?**

    A. 10.25 feet

    B. 15.75 feet

    C. 20.75 feet

    D. 19.25 feet

3. **The Food and Drug Administration requires ice cream to contain which of the following ingredients?**

    A. sugar

    B. chocolate

    C. butterfat

    D. milk

4. **Which of the following is the coldest place in our solar system?**

    A. The North Pole

    B. Pluto

    C. Saturn

    D. Triton

5. When penguins are cold, they turn their backs to the sun. Why?

    A. to increase their body temperature

    B. to get warm faster

    C. to turn away from the wind

    D. to protect their eyes

6. What is the name of the bumps formed on a mountain by the repeated turns of skiers?

    A. mounds

    B. slopes

    C. moguls

    D. lifts

7. On January 23, 1971 Prospect Creek, Alaska, broke the record for the lowest temperature recorded in the U.S. What was the temperature?

    A. -60°F

    B. -58°F

    C. -80°F

    D. -45°F

Answers

1. (A)	3. (C)	5. (B)	7. (C)
2. (B)	4. (D)	6. (C)	

Language Quiz

Q: What does a mnemonic (nih-MAH-nik) device help you do?

A: It helps you remember something. (Mnemonic comes from a Greek word meaning "to remember.")

Q: Which one of these terms is used to define the entire universe? (A) ectoplasm; (B) macrocosm; (C) microcosm; (D) plasma.

A: B (from Greek words makro, which means "large" or "on a wide scale," and kosmos, meaning "world")

Q: Which of these is an example of a palindrome: (A) dark and light; (B) Madam, I'm Adam; (C) stile and style; (D) When will Winnie wake?

A: B (A palindrome is a word or sentence that is spelled the same way backward and forward.)

Q: E is the most commonly used letter in the English language. What is the second most commonly used?

A: T

Q: The aardvark is the first animal listed in the dictionary. What is the last animal listed?

A: Zyzzyva (a tropical weevil)

Q: About how many Amerindian (Native American) languages are still spoken in the U.S.?

A: 175 (Only 20 Amerindian languages are widely used. About 55 may soon disappear, as they are used by just a few elderly speakers.)

Q: Where does the term second string, meaning "replacement" or "backup" come from?

A: It comes from archery. During the Middle Ages, archers carried an extra string in case the one on their bow broke.

Q: If you have musophobia, you have an illogical or exaggerated fear of what?

A: Mice (This fear is also called murophobia and suriphobia.)

Are You a TRENDSETTER?

Some people can really stand out in a crowd, and others are just comfortable being behind the scenes. Find out if you're a trendsetter by taking this quiz!

	LIKE ME	NOT LIKE ME
1. I'm always changing up my look.	◯	◯
2. I don't normally follow the crowd.	◯	◯
3. I don't think about what everyone else is wearing when I look for new clothes.	◯	◯
4. I've been called "stylish" or "cutting edge."	◯	◯
5. I have an eye for design and color.	◯	◯
6. My hairstyle has changed a lot over the years.	◯	◯
7. I love trying new things.	◯	◯
8. I'm really interested in hobbies I've never tried before.	◯	◯

9. My friends come to me for advice on a new look or style.

10. I find fads of the past really interesting.

11. I like to decorate my room and my backpack with things that let people know what music or hobbies I'm into.

12. I'll try things out without judging them first.

13. I like to compliment people when they try something new, like a sport or type of music.

If you answered mostly "Like Me..."

You are most definitely a trendsetter! You're all about creating a unique sense of style, and people look up to that! You aren't concerned with what the crowd is doing; you're more focused on trying new things and mixing it up.

If you answered mostly "Not Like Me..."

You might not be up on the latest trends, but that's totally cool! You're comfortable in your own skin and your interests don't really revolve around fashion or appearance.

Back in the Day

Test your history knowledge by reading the questions and taking a guess at the answers!

Q: What product did Napolean have developed for his army, navy, and the needy people of France?

A: Magarine (In 1869, a chemist named Hippolyte Mége-Mourñés won the prize offered by Napolean for inventing a butter substitute.)

Q: When did Rome become capital of Italy?

A: In 1870

Q: Who was the French citizen, closely associated with George Washington, who fought with the Continental Army during the American Revolution?

A: The Marquis de Lafayette

Q: What famous explorer sailed in a ship called Half Moon?

A: Henry Hudson

Q: Where was the wheelbarrow probably invented?

A: In ancient China (No one knows for sure, but its invention has been credited to Chucko Liang, who lived from 181-234 A.D.)

Q: How did the name "John Hancock" become a slang term for a signature?

A: John Hancock was the first person to sign the Declaration of Independence in 1776. His signature appears first on the page and is the largest.

Q: In ancient Egypt, how did a family mourn when a pet cat died?

A: They shaved their eyebrows.

Q: What 3,000 mile trip did George Samuelson and Frank Harbo complete in a rowboat in 1896?

A: They rowed from New York to England (in 56 days).

Q: How many vessels sailed with Christopher Columbus on his second voyage to the New World?

A: 17

Who's Hungry?

Test your knowledge of food by reading the questions and taking a guess at the answers!

Q: Which vegetable, once called the "mad apple," was long thought to be poisonous?

A: The eggplant

Q: What does the Food and Drug Administration (FDA) require ice cream to contain in order to be called ice cream?

A: At least 10 percent butterfat

Q: What gives a bagel a shiny crust?

A: Before the ring-shaped dough is baked, it is boiled or steamed, then glazed with egg yolk or milk.

Q: The flesh of what vegetable may be purple, yellow, or white?

A: The potato

Q: How much candy do Americans eat in a year?

A: About 7 billion pounds—an average of 24 pounds for every man, woman, and child in the U.S.

Q: What is a love apple?

A: The 19th-century name for a tomato

Q: How can you tell a hard-boiled egg from an uncooked one?

A: Put them side by side and spin them. The one that spins the longest is hard-boiled. (The liquid inside the raw egg sloshes around inside, slowing it down.)

Q: A peanut is not really a nut. What is it?

A: It is a legume (as are peas and beans). A legume is the pod fruit of certain plants, while a nut is a hard dry fruit with a single seed inside.

Q: Which of the following is not a fruit: cucumber, pumpkin, rhubarb, or tomato?

A: Rhubarb (It is an edible leafstalk.)

WEDDING BELLS

Test out your knowledge of weddings with this quiz! The letter of each answer corresponds to a blank in the secret message at the end of the quiz. Get the answers right to uncover the message!

1. In modern times, bridesmaids usually all wear similar dresses. How did this tradition start?

Z. it was the law in ancient civilizations

A. it made it easier for people to stand in the right spot at a wedding

B. as a way to confuse bad spirits

C. weaving the same dresses was a way for wedding guests to bond

2. What country's newlyweds began wearing rings on the third finger of the left hand?

N. Greece

O. China

P. India

Q. Iceland

3. Toasts are popular at weddings. Where did the term "toast" come from?

M. a Moroccan practice of making toast for a new couple

N. an old French way to disguise bad wine with bread

O. traditional weddings use candles to keep guests "toasty"

P. many weddings in the past served breakfast food for guests

4. What is traditionally broken at Italian weddings?

V. bread

W. silverware

X. stones

Y. glass

5. The number of people who get married decreases when _____ becomes scarce.

    L. food   **N.** water

    M. money   **O.** flower

6. What did brides used to carry down the aisle before flowers?

    M. grass   **O.** garlic

    N. feathers   **P.** a sword

7. In the Middle Ages, who was responsible for making the wedding cake?

    O. the guests   **Q.** the groom

    P. the bride   **R.** the king

Answers

1. (B)	3. (N)	5. (M)	7. (O)
2. (N)	4. (Y)	6. (O)	

Where do rabbits go after a wedding?

A __ U __ __ __ __ __ __ N
   (1)   (2) (3) (4) (5) (6) (7)

Answer: A BUNNYMOON

U.S. President Trivia

Test your knowledge of U.S. presidents by reading the questions and taking a guess at the answers!

Q: Who was the only U.S. president elected to two nonconsecutive terms in office?

A: Grover Cleveland (Counted as the 22nd and 24th president, he served from 1885–1889 and 1893–1897.)

Q: What do presidents Grover Cleveland, Abraham Lincoln, Harry S. Truman, and George Washington have in common?

A: They never attended college.

Q: Eight U.S. presidents were born in Virginia—more than in any other state. What state was the birthplace of seven presidents?

A: Ohio

Q: Until 1980, when Ronald Reagan was elected president at age 69, who was the oldest person elected to that office?

A: William Harry Harrison, who was 67 when elected in 1840

Q: Which U.S. president has the most places named after him?

A: George Washington (257 townships, 121 cities and towns, 33 counties, and 1 state)

Q: Who were the first residents of the White House?

A: President John Adams and his wife, Abigail Adams

Q: Who was Abraham Lincoln's running mate when he ran for president in 1860?

A: Hannibal Hamlin

Q: President Ronald Reagan loved jelly beans. During his eight years in office, how much of the candy did the White House buy?

A: About 12 tons

Q: Who is buried in Grant's tomb?

A: Technically, no one. President Ulysses S. Grant and his wife, Julia Dent Grant, are entombed there, in stone coffins in an aboveground chamber. Buried means put in a hole in the ground and covered with earth.

Sporting Around

Do you like playing basketball or tennis with friends? Or maybe you'd rather ride a skateboard or take a jog. Test your knowledge of sports trivia with this multiple-choice quiz. Read each question and see if you can select the correct answer.

1. **Some skateboarders ride on the very front of their skateboards, kicking up the back wheels. What is this called?**

   A. dangerous

   B. nose wheelie

   C. hanging ten

   D. hot-dogging

2. **The average basketball lasts for about how many bounces?**

   A. 10,000

   B. 15,000

   C. 25,000

   D. 1,000

3. **How fast can a tennis ball travel?**

   A. almost 300 miles per hour

   B. almost 75 miles per hour

   C. almost 60 miles per hour

   D. almost 150 miles per hour

4. **In bowling, which is the name given to three strikes in a row?**

   A. a lightning rod

   B. a goose

   C. a turkey

   D. a roll

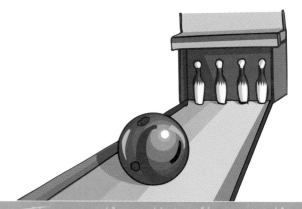

5. The American League originally consisted of eight baseball teams. The first AL games were played in which year?

    A. 1890   **C.** 1920

    B. 1901   **D.** 1930

6. In Olympic badminton, how many feathers must a birdie or shuttlecock have?

    A. 20   **C.** 40

    B. 50   **D.** 16

7. On a regulation basketball court, how high must the hoops be?

    A. 10 feet high   **C.** 12 feet high

    B. 12 feet high   **D.** 8 feet high

8. In 1970, only 127 people ran in the New York City Marathon. In 2003, how many people ran?

    A. 100,210   **C.** 79,820

    B. 34,729   **D.** 201,105

Answers

1. (B)	3. (D)	5. (B)	7. (A)
2. (A)	4. (C)	6. (D)	8. (D)

What's Your Color?

Do you know that color preference says a lot about you? What color best suits you and your personality? Take this quiz to determine your color.

Passionate   Calm   Mysterious

1. The word that best describes me is:
- **A.** Fun
- **B.** Loyal
- **C.** Secretive

2. My favorite season is:
- **A.** Summer
- **B.** Fall
- **C.** Winter

3. When on a team:
- **A.** I am just one of the guys.
- **B.** My plays make others look great.
- **C.** I like to be in charge.

4. Let's talk about fights:
- **A.** I start them.
- **B.** I mediate them.
- **C.** I end them.

5. What kind of pet do you have?
- **A.** Pit bull
- **B.** Beagle
- **C.** Saint Bernard

Passionate—Mostly A's

Your color is definitely red. You are passionate about stuff and go after whatever it is that you want at the moment.

Calm—Mostly B's

Your signature color is blue, for sure. You are calm and peaceful and one of the most loyal guys out there!

Mysterious—Mostly C's

Your signature color is purple, no doubt about it. You have an air of mystery about you and like to live on the edge and crave power.

You're Getting SLEEPY...

Everyone sleeps—people, animals, birds, and even insects. Test your knowledge about sleep with this quiz. Read each question and answer True or False.

TRUE   FALSE

1. It's easy to tell when someone is asleep.

2. It's good to fall asleep as soon as your head hits the pillow.

3. The part of sleep where vivid dreams occur is called REM, or Rapid Eye Movement sleep.

4. Monkeys and apes don't sleep as much as humans.

5. In order to stay aware of danger, ducks will sleep with half of their brain still "awake."

6. It's hard to disrupt a sleeping person.

	TRUE	FALSE

7. Losing some sleep isn't a bad thing. ○ ○

8. Scientists still aren't sure why we dream. ○ ○

9. Horses always sleep standing up. ○ ○

10. The longest period of time a person has been recorded staying awake is eighteen days. ○ ○

Answers

1. False. Some people are capable of sleeping with their eyes open! Professionals can tell when someone is really sleeping.

2. False. Falling asleep right away can mean that you are sleep deprived. If you get enough sleep, it should take you about fifteen minutes to fall asleep.

3. True.

4. False. Our closest relatives, primates, usually sleep ten or more hours at a time.

5. True.

6. False. Even faint light, like the kind from alarm clocks, can interrupt a person's natural sleep cycle even if they don't fully wake up.

7. False. It can be. Sleep deprived people lack focus, and sleep deprivation is a major factor in many car accidents.

8. True.

9. False. Horses can sleep either standing up or lying down—it really depends on the horse!

10. True.

What Does It Mean?

There's a word for just about everything! Test your knowledge of words—and things having to do with words—with this multiple-choice quiz. Read each question and see if you can select the correct answer.

1. What is a group of crows called?

- **A.** gabbers
- **B.** murder
- **C.** howlers
- **D.** pack

2. Warning signs with the words "Cave Canem" were used by ancient Romans. Which does it mean?

- **A.** Stay Away
- **B.** No Entry
- **C.** Keep Off
- **D.** Beware of Dog

3. What does a horologist do?

- **A.** reads horoscopes
- **B.** fixes clocks
- **C.** writes advice columns
- **D.** tells fortunes

4. What does a xenophobe fear?

- **A.** musical instruments
- **B.** foreigners
- **C.** travel
- **D.** butterflies

5. Which word stands for "radio detecting and ranging?"

- **A.** radon
- **B.** radio
- **C.** radar
- **D.** radiator

6. The name Jeep came from the letters GP. They were originally a manufacturer's abbreviation, but what did they eventually stand for?

    A. General Plan   **C.** General Price
    B. General Purpose   **D.** General Practice

7. Which name is given to a group of apes?

    A. herd   **C.** rookery
    B. shrewdness   **D.** colony

8. How many years did it take Noah Webster to compile the first American dictionary in 1828?

    A. 17   **C.** 12
    B. 10   **D.** 5

Answers

1. (B)	3. (B)	5. (C)	7. (B)
2. (D)	4. (B)	6. (B)	8. (A)

A Look at Fast Food

Test out your fast food knowledge with this quiz! The letter of each answer corresponds to a blank in the secret message at the end of the quiz. Get the answers right to uncover the message!

1. Which fast food fare is the most popular in America?

- **J.** hamburgers
- **K.** French fries
- **L.** milkshakes
- **M.** chicken fingers

2. What was sold at the very first fast food stands in ancient Rome?

- **C.** rice and beans
- **D.** poultry and wild game
- **E.** bread and sausages
- **F.** fruit and vegetables

3. Why did fish and chips become a favorite British fast food?

- **T.** better fishing boats became available
- **U.** fried food rose in popularity
- **V.** fish prices dropped
- **W.** there was an abundance of potatoes in England

4. At the drive-in fast food joints of the 1950s, waiters and waitresses got around on _____ while serving people food.

- **C.** roller skates
- **D.** skateboards
- **E.** scooters
- **F.** bicycles

5. Sushi is the go-to Japanese fast food. Some sushi comes in the form of a roll—what typically holds the roll together?

- **E.** mustard
- **F.** flour and water
- **G.** soy sauce
- **H.** dried seaweed

6. Doughnuts are a popular fast food treat. Who were the "doughboys"?

T. master pastry chefs

U. soldiers in World War I

V. servers in a doughnut shop

W. the Dutch, inventors of the doughnut

7. What invention made the milkshake possible?

N. the automated milking machine

O. corn syrup

P. the electric blender

Q. the ice maker

Answers

1. (K)	3. (T)	5. (H)	7. (P)
2. (E)	4. (C)	6. (U)	

What happens when a hamburger misses school?

HE'S GIVEN "__ __ __ __ __ __ __" WORK.
(1) (2) (3) (4) (5) (6) (7)

Q: A male swan is called a cob. A female swan is called a pen. What is a baby swan called?

A: A cygnet (SIG-net)

Q: Does a mosquito have teeth?

A: No, but a mosquito's mouthparts do have sharp, jagged edges that help it pierce the skin.

Q: What type of dog, known to us today, existed in ancient Egypt?

A: The greyhound (A picture of one, on a tomb, dates from about 3000 B.C.)

Q: Which animal has the sharpest sense of hearing: a dog, a dolphin, or a rabbit?

A: A dolphin. Its auditory (hearing) nerve can have 67,900 or more cochlear fibers—twice as many as in the human auditory nerve.

Q: Do all snakes lay eggs?

A: No. Some snake species, such as the garter snake, give birth to live babies.

Q: What bird is the mascot of the U.S. Air Force Academy?

A: The falcon

Q: How far can a flea fly?

A: The flea is a wingless insect. It can't fly, it can only jump.

Q: Each elephant has something that is different from every other elephant—as different as fingerprints are in humans. What is it?

A: The elephant's ears

Q: Which type of elephant, African or Asian, has the larger ears?

A: The African elephant, which is the largest living land animal.

Famous People

1. At age 35, who was one of the youngest people to receive a Nobel Peace Prize?

A. Martin Luther King, Jr.

B. Abraham Lincoln

C. John F. Kennedy

D. Barrack Obama

2. Gandhi was deeply involved in India's struggle for freedom from what powerful island?

A. Japan

B. Jamaica

C. Great Britain

D. Hawaii

3. For which book was author Jonathan Swift best known?

A. *Tom Sawyer*

B. *Gulliver's Travels*

C. *Lord of the Flies*

D. *Wind in the Willows*

4. What is Alexander Graham Bell famous for inventing?

A. printing press

B. light bulb

C. airplane

D. telephone

5. On July 20, 1969, what did U.S. astronaut Neil Armstrong become the first human to do?

    A. travel in a rocket   **C.** set foot on the moon

    B. travel to Mars   **D.** eat food in a rocket

6. Which legendary artist is perhaps best known for his paintings the Last Supper and the Mona Lisa?

    A. Leonardo da Vinci   **C.** Vincent van Gogh

    B. Claude Monet   **D.** Andy Warhol

Answers

1. (A)	3. (B)	5. (C)
2. (C)	4. (D)	6. (A)

AMERICAN

World Facts

Test your knowledge of world trivia with this multiple-choice quiz. Read each question and see if you can select the correct answer.

1. The longest mountain range on Earth is about 10,000 miles long and lies under the Atlantic Ocean, running along the sea floor from Iceland to near the Antarctic Circle. What is it called?

   A. Long Mountain Ridge   **C.** Mid-Atlantic Ridge
   B. Under Sea Ridge   **D.** Antarctic Ridge

2. The Hawaiian Islands were originally named after an earl of England. What were the islands originally known as?

   A. The Prince Charles Islands **C.** The Hamburger Islands
   B. The Sandwich Islands   **D.** The English Muffin Islands

3. The Gobi Desert is the world's largest desert. On which continent is it located?

   A. North America   **C.** Asia
   B. Africa   **D.** Australia

4. Why is the island nation of Sri Lanka known as Gem Island?

   A. there are many colorful   **C.** colorful hummingbirds
   flowers on the islands   live there
   B. a lot of gemstone are   **D.** the sand on the beaches
   found there   is colored like gemstones

5. Which of the Great Lakes lies entirely within the United States and does not border Canada?

    A. Lake Michigan   **C.** Lake Huron

    B. Lake Superior   **D.** Lake Erie

6. Which do more people die from than thirst in the deserts of the southwestern U.S.?

    A. hunger   **C.** drowning in flash floods

    B. heatstroke   **D.** sunburn

7. In which U.S. state would you find Crater Lake?

    A. Washington   **C.** Nevada

    B. Oregon   **D.** Wyoming

8. Where in the U.S. can you find a replica of the famous Parthenon in Greece?

    A. Los Angeles, California   **C.** Nashville, Tennessee

    B. Springfield, Massachusetts   **D.** New Orleans, Louisiana

9. What is the capital of New Zealand?

    A. Auckland   **C.** Nelson

    B. Hamilton   **D.** Wellington

Answers

1. (C)	3. (C)	5. (A)	7. (B)	9. (D)
2. (B)	4. (B)	6. (C)	8. (C)	

Happy Holidays!

Holidays are a time for celebration and different holidays are celebrated in different ways around the world. Test your knowledge of holidays and holiday traditions with this multiple-choice quiz. Read each question and see if you can select the correct answer.

1. In addition to celebrating a new year, Chinese New Year also celebrates what?

A. China's history

B. the collective birthdays of the Chinese people

C. the harvest of annual crops

D. the anniversary of China's rise to power

2. What nation originally celebrated Oktoberfest?

A. France

B. South Africa

C. Australia

D. Germany

3. What day, created in 1970, is said to have kick–started the worldwide environmental movement?

A. Earth Day

B. May Day

C. Arbor Day

D. Mother's Day

4. People in the United States celebrate Thanksgiving to mark when the Pilgrims first landed in Plymouth. What unexpected treat was at the first Thanksgiving?

A. jelly beans

B. watermelon

C. popcorn

D. macaroni and cheese

5. Valentine's Day is a popular holiday around the world. In the Middle Ages, how did sweethearts show their affection for one another?

A. by wearing a sweetheart's name on their sleeve

B. by cooking a huge feast

C. by decorating their horses with hearts

D. by writing elaborate songs

6. Why did people start wearing costumes on Halloween?

A. to scare their neighbors

B. to disguise themselves from evil spirits

C. to show off who had the best sewing skills

D. to enter into costume competitions

7. Cinco de Mayo is an important celebration day in Mexico. When is it celebrated?

A. at harvest time

B. January 1

C. May 5

D. during the first full moon of the year

8. St. Patrick's Day is celebrated in Irish communities all over the world. What is St. Patrick said to have done?

A. saved Ireland from drought

B. driven all the snakes out of Ireland

C. united all the different parts of Ireland

D. granted Ireland bountiful crops

Answers

1. (B) Chinese New Year is often celebrated with parades complete with people manning paper dragons.

2. (D) German immigrants brought the celebration to North America, and it has been recognized there since the 1960s.

3. (A) Earth Day is sometimes celebrated with park cleanups and rallies for environmental causes.

4. (C) The Native Americans taught the Pilgrims to harvest and store corn, helping them survive the winter.

5. (A) Young men would choose names from a bowl and pin the paper to their sleeve. This is where the phrase "wear your heart on your sleeve" comes from.

6. (B) Halloween was originally a religious holiday for the ancient Druids, and they believed evil spirits to be especially active on this night.

7. (C) People celebrate with parades and piñatas, and wear red and green, the colors of the Mexican flag.

8. (B) However, this is only a legend. The climate in Ireland when St. Patrick was alive (around 300 AD) was probably too cold for snakes.

Are You a Foodie?

Q: Popcorn, which is native to the Western Hemisphere, has been eaten by Native Americans for centuries. How old is the oldest known popcorn kernel?

A: At least 1,000 years old

Q: Which part of the strawberry plant is the fruit?

A: Those tiny things on a strawberry's skin that we think of as seeds are the plant's actual fruits.

Q: What vegetable is one of the oldest known crops?

A: Peas

Q: Why does honey give you energy quickly?

A: It is made of two simple sugars that give energy: glucose and fructose. The human body has to break most foods down into these sugars, but in honey, they are ready to go!

Q: What is your favorite school lunch from the cafeteria?

A: According to the American School Food Service Association, pizza is tops with U.S. school kids.

Q: What is the most popular fresh fruit in the U.S.?

A: Bananas. More are sold in the U.S. than any other fruit.

Q: When and where was the world's largest pizza made?

A: On December 8, 1990, in Norwood, South Africa. It measured 122 feet, 8 inches in diameter! Making it took 9,920 pounds of flour; 1,984 pounds of tomato puree; 3, 968 pounds of cheese; and 198 pounds of salt.

In the Kitchen

Read each list of ingredients and guess what tasty recipe is being made.

1. Flour, eggs, butter, sugar, chocolate chips

A. cake

B. pudding

C. chocolate-chip cookies

D. pie

2. Bread, eggs, milk, cinnamon

A. pancakes

B. waffles

C. omelet

D. french toast

3. Tortillas, beef, lettuce, tomatoes, onions

A. hamburgers

B. tacos

C. sandwiches

D. nachos

4. Graham crackers, chocolate, marshmallows

A. chocolate cookies

B. marshmallow crispy treats

C. s'mores

D. graham cracker bars

5. Apples, cinnamon, butter, pie crust

    A. apple muffins   **C.** apple cookies

    B. apple cake   **D.** apple pie

6. Pasta, tomato sauce, onion, ricotta cheese, beef

    A. lasagna   **C.** mozzarella sticks

    B. spaghetti and meatballs   **D.** chicken Parmesan

7. Flour, sugar, milk, eggs, butter, blueberries

    A. brownies   **C.** cinnamon rolls

    B. blueberry muffins   **D.** blueberry pie

8. Toast, bacon, lettuce, tomato, mayonnaise

    A. BLT Sandwich   **C.** grilled cheese

    B. chicken salad sandwich   **D.** hamburger

Answers

1. (C)	3. (B)	5. (D)	7. (B)
2. (D)	4. (C)	6. (A)	8. (A)

This and That

Do you know a little about a lot of different things—that's called trivia. Test your knowledge of trivia with this multiple-choice quiz. Read each question and see if you can select the correct answer.

1. **Before the 1920s what was the color pink associated with?**

   A. dolls

   B. girls

   C. boys

   D. ice cream

2. **Founded in 1859, which was the first modern chain store?**

   A. Walmart

   B. J.C. Penney

   C. Great Atlantic and Pacific Tea Company (A&P)

   D. Woolworth's

3. **How many bathrooms are in the White House?**

   A. 17

   B. 35

   C. 50

   D. 75

4. **What were the names of Cinderella's two mean stepsisters?**

   A. Aurora and Annabelle

   B. Cruella and Ariel

   C. Anastasia and Drizella

   D. Lucifer and Aurora

5. In which month do Canadians celebrate Thanksgiving Day?

    A. January   **C.** November

    B. October   **D.** December

6. To which does the proper name of the famous painting La Giocanda translate:

    A. *Starry Night*   **C.** *Mona Lisa*

    B. *Girl with a Pearl Earring*   **D.** *Whistler's Mother*

7. Which giant sculpture will you find in the town of Vegreville in Alberta, Canada?

    A. dinosaur   **C.** Godzilla

    B. Easter egg   **D.** Statue of Liberty

8. What was the world's first speed limit set for cars in London, England in 1903?

    A. 10 miles per hour   **C.** 20 miles per hour

    B. 60 miles per hour   **D.** 55 miles per hour

Answers

| 1. (C) | 3. (B) | 5. (B) | 7. (B) |
| 2. (C) | 4. (C) | 6. (C) | 8. (C) |

Anatomi-cool Fun

The human body is an amazing machine with many parts. Take this quiz to figure out how much you know about the skin you live in!

1. How many bones do most babies have?

- **A.** 100
- **B.** 200
- **C.** 300
- **D.** 400

2. What is the colorful part of the eye called?

- **A.** iris
- **B.** cornea
- **C.** lash
- **D.** lens

3. A doctor uses _____ to listen to your heart.

- **A.** a thermometer
- **B.** an ultrasound
- **C.** an MRI
- **D.** a stethoscope

4. Cilia line your windpipe. What are they?

- **A.** cells
- **B.** tiny hairs
- **C.** bacteria
- **D.** nerves

5. What does earwax do?

- **A.** keeps the ear clean
- **B.** helps sound travel into the ear
- **C.** keeps loud sounds out
- **D.** holds the ear onto the head

6. Why doesn't it hurt to have your hair cut?

    A. hair is too thin to hurt

    B. hair is too far away from the scalp

    C. hair is just attached to the surface of the skin

    D. hair is made from dead cells

7. Why do you shiver in cold weather?

    A. because your bones shake

    B. because your hair is standing on end

    C. rapid muscle contractions

    D. ice in the blood

8. The right side of the brain controls the _____ of your body.

    A. left side

    B. right side

    C. lower half

    D. upper half

Answers

1. (C)   Adults have 206 bones. Babies' bones fuse over time.

2. (A)   The iris has muscles that help let in or block light from entering the eye.

3. (D)   A healthy heart makes a "lub-dub" sound.

4. (B)   These little hairs prevent you from inhaling dirt and mucus.

5. (A)   Earwax also helps prevent ear infections.

6. (D)   Hair is alive under the skin, at the root.

7. (C)   Your muscles contract in cold weather, causing you to "shake."

8. (A)   No one knows why the brain controls the opposite side of the body!

Creature Feature

Test your animal knowledge by reading the questions and taking a guess at the answers!

1. How tall can a male red kangaroo grow to be?

A. almost 1 foot   **C.** almost 20 feet

B. almost 6 feet   **D.** almost 3 feetl

2. The human body has about 650 muscles. How many muscles does a caterpillar's body have?

A. almost 100   **C.** almost 500

B. 650   **D.** almost 4,000

3. Compsognathus (komp–sog–NAY–thus) is one of the smallest dinosaurs ever found. In terms of size, what can it be compared with?

A. elephant   **C.** chicken

B. horse   **D.** rat

4. What is the average lifespan of a housefly?

A. one year   **C.** one to two hours

B. twenty-four to forty-eight hours   **D.** ten to twenty-one days

5. What species does the bongo from Central Africa belong?

    A. lion   **C.** antelope

    B. giraffe   **D.** aardvark

6. How many eggs can a queen bee lay in one day?

    A. 200   **C.** 20,000

    B. 2,000   **D.** 2 million

7. How long will a young orangutan stay with its mother?

    A. forever   **C.** one year

    B. one month   **D.** seven years

8. What is another name given to a woodchuck or groundhog?

    A. whistle pig   **C.** badger

    B. squirrel   **D.** otter

Answers

1. (B)	3. (C)	5. (C)	7. (D)
2. (D)	4. (D)	6. (B)	8. (A)

Fun with Literature

Test your knowledge of books and their authors with this multiple-choice quiz. Read each question and see if you can select the correct answer.

1. **Which famous author wrote the following books:** *Charlotte's Web*, *Stuart Little*, **and** *The Trumpet of the Swan*?

   A. Charles Dickens

   B. E.B White

   C. A.A Milne

   D. Robert McCloskey

2. **Beatrix Potter is the author of what classic children's book?**

   A. *The Tales of Beatle the Bard*

   B. *Blueberries for Sal*

   C. *The Tale of Peter Rabbit*

   D. *Mother Goose Rhymes*

3. **The Chronicles of Narnia is a seven book fantasy series written by C.S Lewis. What is the name of the first book in the series?**

   A. *The Magician's Nephew*

   B. *Prince Caspian: Return to Narnia*

   C. *The Silver Chair*

   D. *The Lion, the Witch, and the Wardrobe*

4. **What is the best selling book series in history?**

   A. Harry Potter

   B. Goosebumps

   C. Choose Your Own Adventure

   D. Berenstain Bears

5. Which of these books did Dr. Seuss not write?

- **A.** *If I Ran the Zoo*
- **B.** *The Pokey Little Puppy*
- **C.** *Green Eggs and Ham*
- **D.** *Fox in Socks*

6. Which famous author wrote *The Very Hungry Caterpillar?*

- **A.** Margaret Wise Brown
- **B.** Don Freedman
- **C.** Eric Carle
- **D.** Mary Pope Osborne

7. Which of the following books has not been made into a movie?

- **A.** *Alice's Adventures in Wonderland*
- **B.** *Matilda*
- **C.** *Mr. Popper's Penguins*
- **D.** *Tales of a Fourth Grade Nothing*

8. Which famous author wrote the following books: *James and the Giant Peach*, *Charlie and the Chocolate Factory*, and *The BFG?*

- **A.** Louis Sachar
- **B.** Roald Dahl
- **C.** Lois Lowry
- **D.** Laura Ingalls Wilder

Answers

1. (B)	3. (D)	5. (B)	7. (D)
2. (C)	4. (A)	6. (C)	8. (B)

Saving for a
RAINY DAY

The ability to save money is an important skill to learn. How good are you at saving your hard-earned bucks? Take this quiz to find out!

	LIKE ME	NOT LIKE ME
1. When I get my allowance, I plan how to spend it very carefully.	◯	◯
2. I like keeping a record of how much money I have saved.	◯	◯
3. If I see something cool that I'd like to buy, I think about it for a bit before buying.	◯	◯
4. I usually don't borrow money from friends or my parents.	◯	◯
5. I have a piggy bank or coin jar in my room.	◯	◯
6. I'd like to get a part-time job, or summer job, in the future.	◯	◯
7. I don't mind lending a friend some money, as long as they promise to pay me back.	◯	◯
8. I have a few big things I'd like to buy in the long term.	◯	◯

	LIKE ME	NOT LIKE ME
9. I can't really remember buying something I didn't need.	◯	◯
10. I don't mind buying birthday gifts for friends or relatives.	◯	◯
11. If I need to go somewhere to buy something, I don't usually leave the store with unplanned purchases.	◯	◯
12. I like researching things I want to buy to make sure I'm getting the best deal.	◯	◯
13. I take care of my possessions and electronics so I won't need to replace them.	◯	◯
14. I don't mind borrowing books and movies from my local library.	◯	◯
15. I'm not too interested in owning the latest fashion trends or games.	◯	◯

If you answered mostly "Like Me..."

You are an excellent saver! Your money is important to you, but you have a healthy outlook when it comes to buying things you want, either for yourself or for others. You'll find that this skill will come in handy in the future!

If you answered mostly "Not Like Me..."

Sometimes you might not think before you buy something. Even though we all want to own the newest gadgets, games, and clothes, it's important not to spend more than you can handle. Try keeping a journal of money–saving goals and purchases you want to make in the future. Seeing your goals will make them easier to achieve!

How Do You Express Yourself?

Are you a natural leader or more of a go-with-the-flow kind of girl? Take this quiz and find out.

Follower • In Between • Leader

1. **Teacher's conference day is coming up and you're psyched for the day off from school. You're most likely to—**
   - **A.** Scan the newspaper's events section the week before and plan an entire, fun-filled day for you and your friends. (2)
   - **B.** Wait for one of your friends to call you with an idea on how to spend the day. (1)

2. **Your favorite band is coming to the local arena and you think it might be cool to get all your friends together for a party before the concert. You're most likely to—**
   - **A.** Avoid the hassle and just go to the show with a friend or two. Planning a party is too much work! (1)
   - **B.** Dive into the plans headfirst, and make it the most awesome pre-concert bash ever! (2)

3. **Your parents' 20th anniversary is coming up and you would love to throw them a big surprise party. You're most likely to—**
   - **A.** Suggest it to your older siblings, or aunts and uncles, and offer your help in any way possible. (1)
   - **B.** Come up with a plan for the big bash, then take it to your siblings. (2)

4. **You've just learned that a new dress-code rule has been issued at school. You think the rule is totally unfair. You're most likely to—**
   - **A.** Get a group of kids together and start a petition. (2)
   - **B.** Sign any anti-dress code petition that is passed in front of you. (1)

5. **Over the next three Saturday nights, you're most likely to—**
   - **A.** Wait for your buds to let you know what's up. (1)
   - **B.** Call for movie times, then pick a flick for you and your buds to see. (2)

Follower 5-6 points

You're a laid-back and relaxed follower! This is not necessarily a bad thing. You carefully weigh your decisions before diving in.

In-Between 7-8 points

You're a "when the mood strikes" kind of leader! You enjoy taking charge once in a while, and though you may be hesitant to go the distance to take charge, you don't like to sit back and go with the flow.

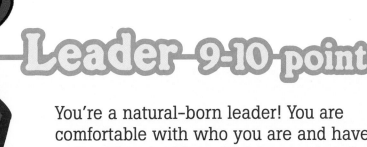

Leader 9-10 points

You're a natural-born leader! You are comfortable with who you are and have no problem looking, thinking, and acting the way you like. You are a trailblazer!

Prepare For TAKEOFF

Airplanes are amazing flying machines! Discover more about them by taking this quiz.

TRUE   FALSE

1. Airplanes constantly spew smoke behind them as they fly.

2. The plane first invented by the Wright brothers is still used as a model for modern planes.

3. Mercury is banned on flights because even a small amount can damage the aluminum from which an airplane is made.

4. Your ears pop on a flight due to a change in the air pressure in the plane. Yawning or swallowing can get rid of the pressure.

5. Flying near lightning is extremely dangerous.

6. Doors on an airplane must be locked securely so that they don't pop open during flight.

7. Modern airplanes have become so automated that the most work a pilot does is during takeoff and landing.

8. A jet engine may burn 1,000 or more gallons of fuel per hour.

9. New airplanes are tested by designers by making models before they are actually built.

10. The longest recorded flight of a paper airplane is 20.9 seconds.

Answers

1. False. The "smoke" is actually water vapor. The amount of water vapor that is visible changes with how high or low the plane is flying.

2. False. The Wright brothers' plane was built from wood and only flew for about 12 seconds.

3. True.

4. True.

5. False. Airplanes contain a device that protects against surges of electricity, and the plane's metal exterior keeps everyone inside from getting zapped.

6. False. Though doors have a safety lock, the higher the plane goes, the harder the pressure from the outside becomes. It would be extremely hard for a door to be opened mid-flight.

7. True.

8. True.

9. True.

10. True.

FUN WITH FABLES

Fables are stories that usually include animals and end in a valuable lesson, or moral. Do any of these fables below sound familiar? See if you can fill in the blanks!

1. The hare thought he could beat the _____ in a _____. All along the way, the hare rested and even took a _____ and he lost track of time! The _____ continued at his own pace and _____. He proved that slow but _____ wins the _____!

2. A lion was woken up by a mouse. He was very _____ —he was enjoying a nap! The mouse _____ged for the lion to let him go, and the lion did. Later, the lion was caught in a big _____. The mouse, remembering the lion's kindness, _____ed through the ropes. _____ friends may prove to be great friends.

3. On a summer day, a grasshopper came across an ant. The ant was _____ing hard to _____ for winter. The grasshopper told the ant to relax and have some _____. Once winter came, the grasshopper had no _____, and the ant had plenty to eat. It is best to be _____ed.

4. A beautiful peacock came upon a crane who was very

_____. The peacock laughed, "My _____ are so

colorful and yours are just white!" The crane replied, "That's true,

but I can _____ far above the earth, while you stay close to

the _____ , like a common rooster." Fine feathers don't make

fine _____.

5. A shepherd boy was watching over his flock of _____.

He was very _____ and decided to entertain himself. He ran

into town yelling "_____!" When help arrived, there was no

danger to be found. One day, a wolf appeared and the boy ran for

_____. The people didn't believe him, and the wolf ate up

all his _____. No one will _____ a liar, even when they

speak the _____.

Something's Fishy

Fish fill the sea! There's a ton to learn about these slippery creatures. Take this quiz to see how much you know!

1. What keeps fish afloat?

- **A.** their fins
- **B.** an air bladder
- **C.** gills and scales
- **D.** air bubbles

2. A fish's body temperature changes with the temperature of the air around them. What does this make them?

- **A.** cold-blooded
- **B.** herbivorous
- **C.** warm-blooded
- **D.** mammals

3. Some species of fish move in large groups called _____.

- **A.** teams
- **B.** herds
- **C.** crowds
- **D.** schools

4. What fish gets its name from its bright, colorful markings?

- **A.** rainbow fish
- **B.** silverfish
- **C.** clownfish
- **D.** dart fish

5. Which of the following is NOT a fish?

- **A.** whale shark
- **B.** barracuda
- **C.** starfish or sea star
- **D.** sea horse

6. What is the world's fastest fish?

- **A.** great white shark
- **B.** sailfish
- **C.** tiger shark
- **D.** eel

7. Baby Pacific salmon work together with what animals?

    A. bears   **C.** moose

    B. flies   **D.** beavers

8. Bluefin tuna are a prized ingredient for _____.

    A. pasta   **C.** chowder

    B. sushi   **D.** fish sticks

9. Goldfish are popular pets. What do baby goldfish lack that adult goldfish have?

    A. their color   **C.** their gills

    B. their eyes   **D.** their tails

Answers

1. (B) Some fish, like sharks, lack an air bladder and must constantly swim to keep from sinking.

2. (A) Most reptiles, like turtles and lizards, are cold-blooded, too.

3. (D) A school can contain 100 or more fish.

4. (C) Clownfish live in sea anemones—they're immune to the anemone's stings.

5. (C) Starfish, or sea stars, use tiny feet on their underside to move around.

6. (B) Sailfish have been clocked at 68 miles per hour (110 km/hour).

7. (D) Baby salmon use beaver dams to grow up hidden from predators.

8. (B) Bluefin tuna are considered so delicious that they are being overfished.

9. (A) Goldfish's color builds as they grow older.

Do You Have Good Manners?

Are you polite or are you a little bit too rude? To find out, read each statement, then put a check under "True" or "False." When you're done, go to the end of the quiz to see your results!

TRUE   **FALSE**

1. I try not to be too loud.

2. I cover my mouth when I cough.

3. I use a tissue or handkerchief when I sneeze.

4. I don't litter.

5. I always knock on a door before I enter a room.

6. I try my best never to insult people.

7. I never interrupt people when they are talking.

	TRUE	FALSE
8. I always use silverware, not my hands, to eat.	◯	◯
9. Words like "sorry" and "thank you" are a big part of my vocabulary.	◯	◯
10. I always respect my elders.	◯	◯
11. I never use foul language.	◯	◯

POLITE DUDE

If you chose mostly "True" answers, you are a polite guy, which is a good thing. People tend to gravitate toward people who are polite to them, because they feel comfortable around them. Keep it up.

RUDE AND CRUDE

If you chose mostly "False" answers, you're a little on the rude side. Try to tone it down and adopt some better manners. You'll be surprised what a difference it makes.

Fascinating Science Facts

Do you enjoy learning about science? Test your science knowledge with this multiple-choice quiz. Read each question and see if you can select the correct answer.

1. **The longest period without rain lasted fourteen years, from October 1903 to January 1918. It happened in which of these places:**

    A. Durban, South Africa   **C.** Sydney, Australia

    B. Nevada, U.S.A.   **D.** Arica, Chile

2. **A storm is considered a hurricane when the winds reach which speed?**

    A. 64 miles per hour   **C.** 74 miles per hour

    B. 55 miles per hour   **D.** 101 miles per hour

3. **What is the only mammal that can fly?**

    A. bat   **C.** mouse

    B. squirrel   **D.** owl

4. **Poison oak is not in the oak family and poison ivy is not in the ivy family. They both belong in which family?**

    A. peanut   **C.** cashew

    B. walnut   **D.** almond

5. Acid rain is formed when rain mixes with which substance?

    A. industrial pollution   **C.** sand

    B. acid   **D.** dust

6. Saturn is not the only planet in our solar system that has rings. Which planets have also been found to have rings?

    A. Earth, Mars, Jupiter   **C.** Mercury, Mars, Earth

    B. Venus, Mercury, Uranus   **D.** Uranus, Jupiter, Neptune

7. Which of our planets is the only one not named for an ancient god?

    A. Saturn   **C.** Earth

    B. Mercury   **D.** Mars

8. How many Earths could fit in the sun?

    A. one thousand   **C.** one hundred

    B. one million   **D.** one billion

Answers

1. (D)	3. (A)	5. (A)	7. (C)
2. (C)	4. (C)	6. (D)	8. (B)

Are You an Introvert or an Extrovert?

Read each statement, and then put a check under "Like Me" or "Not Like Me." When you're done, go to the end of the quiz to find out your personality type!

	LIKE ME	NOT LIKE ME
1. I wear lots of bright colors.		
2. I prefer calling my friends instead of texting them.		
3. I like doing homework in a quiet place, like the library.		
4. I usually hang out with small groups of people.		
5. When my friends and I go to the movies, I usually pick what we see.		
6. In school, I prefer working individually instead of in groups.		
7. I always raise my hand before saying something in class.		
8. If I have a crush, I tell everyone I know about it!		

9. My friends are always asking me for advice.

10. I would rather be treasurer than class president.

11. I always ask for solos in music class.

12. Sometimes I get in trouble for talking during study hall.

13. I've always had more best friends than acquaintances.

14. I never get nervous before giving a presentation in class.

15. I like to make my plans for the weekend early in the week.

Tally it up!

If you chose mostly "Like Me" you're not afraid to speak your mind and get involved with social events. Some people even call you a "Social Butterfly"!

If you chose mostly "Not Like Me" answers, you are an introvert! You tend to get the most fun out of doing low-key events with a small group of people instead of a crowd. You make and maintain strong relationships with your close group of friends.

That's Entertainment!

Test your knowledge of movies, music, and more by reading the questions and taking a guess at the answers!

Q: What was the motto of the Three Musketeers?

A: "All for one and one for all!"

Q: What fictional character is known as the "boy who wouldn't grow up"?

A: Peter Pan, from a 1904 play by James M. Barrie called *Peter Pan, the Boy Who Wouldn't Grow Up*

Q: In the classic Bugs Bunny cartoon *Rabbit Hood*, the Sheriff of Nottingham catches Bugs doing what?

A: Taking carrots from the king's garden

Q: What type of dragon did Viktor Krum face in book four of the Harry Potter series?

A: A Chinese Fireball (in *Harry Potter and the Goblet of Fire* by J. K. Rowling)

Q: Can you name all the dwarfs in the movie *Snow White and the Seven Dwarfs*?

A: Bashful, Doc, Dopey, Grumpy, Happy, Sleepy, and Sneezy

Q: Street names from a real place were used in the original version of the Monopoly board game. What is the city?

A: Atlantic City, New Jersey

Q: In *The Wizard of Oz*, who wanted Dorothy's shoes?

A: The Wicked Witch of the West

Q: Match the superhero with his secret identity:
1. Barry Allen, police scientist   A. Daredevil
2. Bruce Banner, scientist   B .The Flash
3. Hal Jordan, test pilot   C. The Green Lantern
4. Matt Murdock, lawyer   D. The Incredible Hulk

A: 1–B; 2–D; 3-C; 4–A

Q: In the Harry Potter books, what is the animal shop in Diagon Alley called?

A: Magical Menagerie

Back in the Day

1. Where was glass first made?

    A. Sweden   **C.** Egypt

    B. China   **D.** England

2. Who was the first woman to appear on U.S. currency?

    A. Sacajawea   **C.** Harriet Tubman

    B. Susan B. Anthony   **D.** Helen Keller

3. Which was the first company to issue a credit card in 1950?

    A. American Express   **C.** Diner's Club

    B. Mastercard   **D.** Visa

4. Where was the first shopping mall, the Country Club Plaza, founded in 1922?

    A. Flint, Michigan   **C.** Chicago, Illinois

    B. Kansas City, Missouri   **D.** Milwaukee, Wisconsin

5. **Where was the first shot of the American Revolution, known as "the shot heard 'round the world," fired on April 19, 1775?**

    A. Savannah, South Carolina   **C.** Lexington, Massachusetts

    B. Brooklyn, New York   **D.** Philadelphia, Pennsylvania

6. **In which state was the world's first successful oil well drilled?**

    A. Texas   **C.** Pennsylvania

    B. California   **D.** Utah

7. **What was the price of the Louisiana Territory when President Thomas Jefferson bought it from France in 1803?**

    A. $1 per acre   **C.** $5 per acre

    B. 10¢ per acre   **D.** 2¢ per acre

8. **Which famous American landmark had its official opening in 1931?**

    A. Sears Tower   **C.** Empire State Building

    B. Wings   **D.** Capitol Building

Answers

1. (C)	3. (C)	5. (C)	7. (D)
2. (B)	4. (B)	6. (C)	8. (C)

Fruits or Veggies?

Fruits and vegetables are necessities! Some people prefer fruit, and some people like veggies best—what's your favorite? Take this quiz to find out—your results may give you some new meal ideas!

1. When is your favorite time to eat?
- **A.** In the morning
- **B.** I like to snack throughout the day.
- **C.** The early evening

2. What is your favorite season?
- **A.** Spring or summer
- **B.** Fall or winter
- **C.** I like something about each season!

3. How would you describe your wardrobe?
- **A.** A mix of tops and bottoms, and a variety of color options
- **B.** Mostly the same kinds of outfits. I have certain colors I like.
- **C.** I have a few favorite items that I like to mix and match.

4. You're a little nervous about getting on a roller coaster—how do you handle it?
- **A.** I try it! It can't be that bad.
- **B.** I don't know . . . it's really scary . . .
- **C.** As long as it's not too fast, I might try it.

5. What's your go-to Halloween costume?
- **A.** I don't have one!
- **B.** A ghost or vampire
- **C.** A character from the latest scary movie

3. What's your favorite thing to do at the beach?
- **A.** I like to surf or boogie board.
- **B.** Play in the sand
- **C.** Take a dip then lounge around

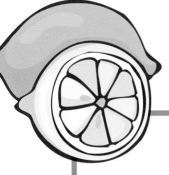

Mostly A's

Fruits

The mostly sweet, sometimes surprising, and overall flavors of fruit really fit your personality. Try eating fruit along with other things—in salads, in smoothies, or together with other fruits. You won't be afraid to try new combinations.

Mostly B's

Vegetables

Not everyone likes veggies but you're a true fan! Vegetables go well with other things because they can have mild flavors. Step out of the box and try mixing vegetables with fruits in a smoothie, or create a spicy marinade to give those veggies some zip!

Mostly C's

You Mix it Up

You love a wide variety of fruits and veggies. Stir-fries, salads, salsas, and chutneys would all suit you very well. Sweet and sour might be one of your favorite flavors. Try to branch out by adding some new spices to your already wild creations!

What's Your Future Career?

The future holds endless possibilities. You can do or be anything you want! Take this quiz to determine your future career.

Builder   Designer   Problem-Solver

1. You're bored. What do you do?
- **A.** Gather bits and pieces of anything from around the house and build a robot.
- **B.** Grab my markers and draw the finest piece of graffiti known to man.
- **C.** Patrol the neighborhood to see if anyone needs my help with anything.

2. Your personal hero is:
- **A.** Frank Gehry
- **B.** Vincent Van Gogh
- **C.** Albert Einstein

3. Your prized possession is:
- **A.** My hammer
- **B.** My graphics programs
- **C.** My pretend badge

4. What's your dream vacation destination?
- **A.** Prague, to check out the architecture
- **B.** Paris, to visit all the museums
- **C.** New York City, to see the 9/11 Memorial

5. What's your favorite type of TV show?
- **A.** Home improvement shows—I love to see what they build.
- **B.** Cartoons—they have the most awesome graphics.
- **C.** True crime, all the way!

Builder—Mostly A's

You love to build stuff—you probably have all kinds of awesome tools. Your future career will be in architecture, where you can plan the building of structures or in actual construction, where you can be hands-on and do the building yourself.

Designer—Mostly B's

You dig designing and drawing and love to appreciate others' creations, too. Your future career will be in graphic design or illustration. You'll design totally cool video games or cartoons or books and magazines.

Problem-Solver—Mostly C's

You love to get to the bottom of a problem and to rescue people in trouble. Your future career will be in law enforcement as a police officer or a detective, or in firefighting. You'll be able to help people in need and solve crimes every day of your life.

Body of Knowledge

The human body is a complex, working machine! Test your knowledge of the human body with this multiple-choice quiz. Read each question and see if you can select the correct answer.

1. Which person has more hair per square inch?

    A. someone with red hair   **C.** someone with blond hair

    B. someone with brown hair   **D.** someone with black hair

2. About 10 percent of the world's population is which?

    A. blond   **C.** brown-eyed

    B. left-handed   **D.** tall

3. How many calories must a human body burn to work off a single pound of fat?

    A. 100   **C.** 3,500

    B. 35   **D.** 350

4. The average person drinks about 16,000 gallons of which liquid in a lifetime?

    A. coffee   **C.** orange juice

    B. water   **D.** cola

5. About 75 percent of the human brain is made up of which?

    A. fat   **C.** water

    B. muscle   **D.** memory

6. Which part of the human body has no sweat glands?

    A. lips   **C.** feet

    B. legs   **D.** hands

7. Which describes the malady called furfur?

    A. excessive amounts of hair   **C.** dandruff

    B. baldness   **D.** curly-haired

8. Which does the average person do 4.2 million times a year?

    A. take a breath   **C.** blink

    B. eat   **D.** complain

Answers

1. (C)	3. (C)	5. (C)	7. (C)
2. (B)	4. (B)	6. (A)	8. (C)

Leisure Time Quiz

Everyone deserves a break sometimes. There are many ways to enjoy time off. Test your knowledge of trivia relating to leisure with this multiple-choice quiz. Read each question and see if you can select the correct answer.

1. **Which final episode of a television show holds the record for largest audience?**

   A. *Friends*

   B. *M*A*S*H*

   C. *E.R.*

   D. *The Bob Newhart Show*

2. **Which was the "planet" in the book and movies, *The Planet of the Apes*?**

   A. Mars

   B. Earth

   C. Saturn

   D. Jupiter

3. **Which was the first thing Clark Kent took off before changing into Superman?**

   A. shirt

   B. tie

   C. glasses

   D. watch

4. **How many letter tiles are there in a game of Scrabble?**

   A. 50

   B. 100

   C. 75

   D. 26

5. Which was the first manuscript to be produced on a typewriter?

    A. *Gone with the Wind*   **C.** *Tom Sawyer*
    B. *Through the Looking Glass*   **D.** *To Kill a Mockingbird*

6. Which film star lost a Charlie Chaplin look–alike contest?

    A. Brad Pitt   **C.** Robert Downey, Jr.
    B. Charlie Chaplin   **D.** Leonardo DiCaprio

7. In *The Lord of the Rings*, what is Gollum's real name?

    A. Smeagol   **C.** Thorin
    B. Slytherin   **D.** Voldemort

8. Which song is film star Gene Autry famous for recording?

    A. "It's a Grand Old Flag"   **C.** "What a Wonderful World"
    B. "Happy Birthday"   **D.** "Rudolph the Red-nosed Reindeer"

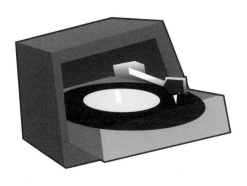

Answers

1. (B)   3. (C)   5. (C)   7. (A)

2. (B)   4. (B)   6. (B)   8. (D)

Facts in BLOOM

The flowers around us are so diverse! Find out about these pretty plants with this quiz.

	TRUE	FALSE
1. Roses are related to some fruits like peaches and apples, and nuts like almonds.	○	○
2. Sunflowers move throughout the day to better soak up sun at different times.	○	○
3. Flowers only bloom in the presence of sunlight.	○	○
4. All flowers have a pleasing scent.	○	○
5. The word daisy is a shortened form of "day's eye," once called this because its center is as bright as the sun.	○	○
6. Flowers are a fairly recent development on Earth.	○	○

7. Saffron, a highly expensive spice, comes from the crocus flower.

8. Honey can be found in the center of a flower.

9. Lilies are prized for their medicinal value.

10. Tulip bulbs are edible and some people in Japan grind them into flour.

Answers

1. True.

2. True.

3. False. Evening primroses and moon flowers are just some of the flowers that bloom ONLY at night.

4. False. The corpse flower, a giant type of lily, is said to smell like rotting meat. It is also the largest known flower.

5. True.

6. False. Flowers, as we know them today, existed 150 million years ago.

7. True.

8. False. Bees need to process a flower's nectar into honey.

9. False. Though people in Elizabethan England used lilies to clean wounds and cure fever, the lily actually has no medical benefit.

10. True.

Animal Antics

Test your knowledge of animals with this multiple-choice quiz. Read each question and see if you can select the correct answer.

1. Which can a cockroach live about a week without?

    A. legs   **C.** head

    B. antennae   **D.** abdomen

2. Worldwide, there are about 2,500 species of which?

    A. dogs   **C.** ants

    B. mosquitoes   **D.** flies

3. How many teeth does an adult dog have?

    A. 12   **C.** 42

    B. 22   **D.** 20

4. Which is the largest type of bear?

    A. sun bear   **C.** black bear

    B. grizzly bear   **D.** kodiak bear

5. Which animal's name means "earth pig"?

    A. anteater   **C.** boar

    B. aardvark   **D.** hog

6. How does the honeybee communicate?

    A. buzzing sounds   **C.** stinging

    B. flapping wings   **D.** distinctive dances

7. The capybara, which lives in Central and South America, can grow to be 4 feet long and weigh up to 100 pounds. It is the largest animal of which family?

    A. cat   **C.** rodent

    B. prairie dog   **D.** pig

8. How many species of fish are there?

    A. 200   **C.** 20 million

    B. 20,000   **D.** 200,000

Answers

1. (C)	3. (C)	5. (B)	7. (B)
2. (B)	4. (D)	6. (D)	8. (C)

The Story of Animation

Have you ever wondered how cartoons got their start? Take this quiz about the history of animation to find out!

1. **What was the first version of animation as we know it today?**

   A. the flip book
   B. the projector
   C. the photograph
   D. the phonograph

2. **Before 1900, most cartoons were**

   A. very short
   B. very long
   C. easy to make
   D. realistic

3. **Whose job is it to match sounds and voices with animation?**

   A. editor
   B. sound engineer
   C. composer of the soundtrack
   D. voice actor

4. **In the 1930s, how were some animation companies able to produce multiple, full-length cartoon films?**

   A. by reusing multiple scenes
   B. by hiring many animators
   C. by making the credits of the movie extra long
   D. by not coloring in the animations

5. **The number of kids who watch Saturday morning cartoons declined in the 1980s. Why?**

   A. cartoons became boring
   B. animators quit their jobs
   C. the video tape became available
   D. parents gave kids more chores

6. Which of the below is a form of animation?

    A. chalkmation   **C.** speedy animation

    B. claymation   **D.** drawmation

7. What is often considered the biggest advancement in animation in recent years?

    A. the ballpoint pen   **C.** improved animation schools

    B. erasable ink   **D.** the computer

Answers

1. (A) Flip books were children's toys—each page showed a single image and when flipped quickly, the images seemed to move.

2. (D) In 1902, George Méliès created a cartoon that involved a spaceship visiting the "man in the moon." This marked a move into the wild imaginations of cartoonists.

3. (B) The sound engineer separates a voice actor's words into different sounds to better match the animation. "Hello" has two sounds, "he" and "llo."

4. (A) Animators used celluloid, a clear kind of paper, to trace over and tweak backgrounds, scenes, and even some characters.

5. (C) Once the videotape went on the market, kids could watch cartoons whenever they wanted and they soon became less interested in the ones on TV.

6. (B) Clay characters are moved slightly and a single frame is shot. The process repeats many, many times and the shots are shown in sequence, appearing animated.

7. (D) The first totally computer animated movie was *Toy Story*, released in 1995. They have been wildly popular since then.

The Fascinating Body

Test your knowledge of the human body by reading the questions and taking a guess at the answers!

Q: What human organ weighs an average of 9 ounces in males and 10.5 ounces in females, and is about the size of a fist?

A: The heart

Q: What body part grows about one-third more slowly than fingernails?

A: Toenails

Q: How many times do you blink your eyes in a year?

A: 4.2 million

Q: What can cause a person to lose up to two quarts of sweat?

A: Working and exercising in warm and humid conditions

Q: What part of the upper body is impossible for you to lick?

A: Your elbow

Q: What cells die out and are replaced by new ones every seven to ten days?

A: Taste receptor cells on the tongue

Q: How many tons of food does the average American adult eat in one year?

A: One ton a year, or an average of 77 tons in a lifetime

Q: There are 270 bones in most babies at birth. How many bones do most adults have?

A: 206; As you grow, smaller bones fuse together to form larger bones.

WHAT DO YOU KNOW

About Animals?

Test your knowledge of animals and their behaviors with this multiple-choice quiz. Read each question and see if you can select the correct answer.

1. What do the emu, kiwi, ostrich, and penguin all have in common?

    A. they live in the Antarctica   **C.** they are becoming extinct

    B. they cannot fly   **D.** they all lay five eggs at a time

2. What is an attribute of the tiny red-billed quelea?

    A. it is the smallest bird known   **C.** it has the greatest living population of any bird

    B. it is the rarest bird known

    D. it does not lay eggs

3. Which spider has a harmless bite to humans?

    A. rattlesnake   **C.** cobra

    B. wolf spider   **D.** coral snake

4. Which insect has the loudest call?

    A. African cicada   **C.** cricket

    B. grasshopper   **D.** bumblebee

5. Which of these creatures has the best memory?

    A. dog   **C.** mouse

    B. rat   **D.** cat

6. **Which animal has the largest brain in proportion to its size?**

    A. butterfly   **C.** ant

    B. hamster   **D.** housefly

7. **Which of the following animals can gain 7 pounds in an hour?**

    A. baby giraffe   **C.** bear cub

    B. baby blue whale   **D.** lion cub

8. **Which is the smallest mammal in the world?**

    A. hummingbird   **C.** bumblebee bat

    B. mouse   **D.** hamster

9. **What age is a camel considered fully mature?**

    A. 6 to 8 years old   **C.** 1 month old

    B. 1 year old   **D.** 10 years old

Answers

1. (B)	3. (B)	5. (D)	7. (B)	9. (A)
2. (C)	4. (A)	6. (C)	8. (C)	

What Should You Do During Your Summer Vacation?

It's no secret that summer vacation is fun, but have you ever thought of the best way to spend your summer? Figure out your ideal summer activity—something that fits your personality—by taking this quiz.

1. **Your mom asks you to help out with a big family party. What do you volunteer to do?**
   A. I can run errands and pick up stuff at the store.
   B. I'd be good at organizing and setting up the table, and maybe decorating.
   C. I can help prepare some food and make sure the house is super clean.

2. **Which of the following is something you participate in after school, or is something you'd like to try?**
   A. Amnesty International
   B. Outdoor sports like track, soccer, or tennis
   C. Junior Honor society or volunteering

3. **What would you consider your ultimate getaway destination?**
   A. Somewhere I've never been before, maybe a faraway place
   B. Hiking, camping—anything outdoors
   C. Somewhere with a lot of new people to meet

4. **Your best friend is disappointed about losing his or her game today. What do you do?**
   A. Pick up his or her favorite video game and relax with some snacks.
   B. Tell him or her that for the next twenty-four hours, they can do whatever they want.
   C. Offer to take him or her out for a movie and some food.

5. **The next town over has been out of power for days and is asking for help. What do you do?**
   A. Go to the town and ask them what they need.
   B. Help load up supplies heading to the town.
   C. Organize a donation campaign at home.

Mostly A's
Take a Trip

You love visiting strange places and can adapt to new situations quickly. You're destined to be a world traveler, and summer vacation is a perfect time to visit somewhere you've never been before!

Mostly B's
Summer Camp

Your personality is best suited for teaching and helping others. Summer camp is a great way to sharpen the skills you already have. You may find yourself tutoring or teaching in the future, and your summer experience will have you prepped!

Mostly C's
Volunteer

You're a compassionate person who is always looking to help someone in need. Volunteering is easy and fun—see if there are places like food banks in your area, and spend the summer giving back to the community!

Red, White, and Blue

Test your knowledge of the United States by reading the questions and taking a guess at the answers!

Q: When did Native Americans officially become U.S. citizens?

A: In 1924, when the Indian Citizenship Act became law

Q: In what year was the first Easter egg roll held on the White House lawn?

A: 1878 (Before then, Easter egg rolls were held on the grounds of the U.S. Capitol.)

Q: Which U.S. war is associated with the slogan "Remember the Maine"?

A: The Spanish-American War of 1898 (The Maine was a U.S. battleship that was sunk in the harbor at Havana, Cuba, on January 15, 1898.)

Q: What city was the first in the U. S. to establish a police department?

A: Boston, Massachusetts

Q: In 1630, John Winthrop changed the name of the Massachusetts settlement of Shawmut to what?

A: Boston

Q: On January 10, 1776, Thomas Paine published a pamphlet that became the battle cry for American independence. What was it called?

A: *Common Sense*

Q: What two Native American tribes are the only ones to have signed an official peace treaty with the U.S.?

A: The Miccosukee and the Seminole

Q: What is the only building to appear on two different U.S. notes of currency—the $2 bill and the $100 bill?

A: Independence Hall (The back of the $2 bill shows the signing of the Declaration of Independence, which took place inside the building. The back of the $100 bill shows the building's exterior.)

WHAT DO YOU KNOW

About Science?

Test your knowledge of science with this multiple-choice quiz. Read each question and see if you can select the correct answer.

1. **What did Edwin Land, inventor of the Polaroid camera, also invent?**

    A. iPod

    B. video camera

    C. polarized sunglasses

    D. cell phones

2. **What is the originally named "clasp locker" known as now?**

    A. velcro

    B. zipper

    C. buttons

    D. snaps

3. **Garrett Augustus Morgan invented two lifesaving devices. One was the gas mask. Which was the other?**

    A. the life jacket

    B. the seatbelt

    C. the traffic light

    D. the airbag

4. **The Explorer 1 was the first man-made one of which of the following, launched successfully by the U.S. in 1958?**

    A. rocket

    B. cannon

    C. hot air balloon

    D. satelite

5. Which practical household item was invented in 1830?

    A. toaster   **C.** lawnmower

    B. microwave oven   **D.** coffee maker

6. What does a nematologist study?

    A. skin   **C.** heartworms

    B. roundworms   **D.** dust

7. What does a botanist study?

    A. human anatomy   **C.** planets

    B. plants   **D.** animals

8. What falls to Earth from meteors and other space bodies and causes Earth's weight to increase by about 90 tons per day?

    A. sand   **C.** water

    B. glass particles   **D.** dust

Answers

1. (C)	3. (C)	5. (C)	7. (B)
2. (B)	4. (D)	6. (B)	8. (D)

Famous Women

Test your knowledge of famous women with this multiple-choice quiz.

1. **Who was the first woman to win a Nobel Prize?**

   A. Annie Oakley   **C.** Mother Teresa

   B. Marie Curie   **D.** Susan B. Anthony

2. **Which famous author is known for writing the following books: *Tales of a Fourth Grade Nothing, Are You There God? It's Me, Margaret*, and *The One in the Middle is the Green Kangaroo*?**

   A. J.K. Rowling   **C.** Judy Blume

   B. Louisa May Alcott   **D.** Sharon Creech

3. **Who is credited with the following quote: "No one can make you feel inferior without your consent"?**

   A. Eleanor Roosevelt   **C.** Hillary Clinton

   B. Marilyn Monroe   **D.** Condoleezza Rice

4. **Who acted as an interpreter and guide for explorers Lewis & Clark as they explored the western United States?**

   A. Abigail Adams   **C.** Sojourner Truth

   B. Laura Ingalls Wilder   **D.** Sacagawea

5. **Jane Goodall is considered the foremost expert on what animal?**

   A. lions   **C.** chimpanzees

   B. iguanas   **D.** grizzly bears

6. Venus and Serena Williams are known as champions of what sport?

   A. ice-skating   **C.** basketball

   B. tennis   **D.** softball

7. Who was the first American woman to travel into space?

   A. Oprah Winfrey   **C.** Shirley Temple

   B. Sandra Day O'Connor   **D.** Sally Ride

8. Known as a civil rights leader, which American woman is most famous for refusing to give up her bus seat to a white man?

   A. Rosa Parks   **C.** Helen Keller

   B. Amelia Earhart   **D.** Harriet Tubman

Answers

1. (B)   Maire Curie won the Nobel Prize for Physics in 1903.

2. (C)   In total, Judy Blume has written 27 books.

3. (A)   Eleanor Roosevelt was married to the 32nd president of the United States, Franklin D. Roosevelt.

4. (D)   Sacagawea's face is remembered on the U.S. one dollar coin.

5. (C)   Jane Goodall has studied chimpanzees for over 45 years.

6. (B)   Venus and Serena Williams have each won four Olympic Gold medals.

7. (D)   Sally Ride traveled into space in 1983.

8. (A)   Rosa Parks' actions led to the Montgomery Bus Boycott in 1955.

General Knowledge

Q: What was the first automobile mass-produced in the U.S.?

A: The Oldsmobile, manufactured by Ransome Eli Olds in 1901. (About 12 years later, Henry Ford invented an improved assembly-line process.)

Q: What is the main use, by humans, of squirrel hairs?

A: They are used to make camel-hair paintbrushes. The brushes are also made with goat, pony, and ox hair, but not with hair from camels.

Q: What is the most common surname in the world?

A: Chang

Q: Where does the saying "Don't count your chickens before they are hatched" come from?

A: An Aesop's fable

Q: How many dollar bills, laid lengthwise end to end, would it take to encircle Earth at the equator?

A: 256,964,529 dollar bills (Earth's circumference at the equator: 24,901.55 miles; a dollar bill's length: 6.14 inches)

Q: During what century is Robin Hood said to have robbed from the rich and given to the poor?

A: The 12th century

Q: Whose heart beats faster: an adult human's or an elephant's?

A: An adult human's (adult human's heart: 70 to 80 beats per minute; elephant's heart: about 25 beats per minute)

Medical Firsts

The medical field is always changing as new discoveries and innovations are made. Take a look at some historic medical firsts with this quiz.

1. During the first successful open heart surgery, how long did the patient go without a beating heart?

- **A.** 5 minutes
- **B.** 10 minutes
- **C.** 20 minutes
- **D.** 30 minutes

2. For what illness was the first vaccine created?

- **A.** smallpox
- **B.** chicken pox
- **C.** influenza
- **D.** cholera

3. What society produced the first known female doctor?

- **A.** ancient Egypt
- **B.** ancient Rome
- **C.** the Druids
- **D.** feudal Japan

4. What unexpected object appeared on the world's first X-ray?

- **A.** a lizard
- **B.** a chicken bone
- **C.** a ring
- **D.** a flower

5. What was the first animal to be cloned?

- **A.** a toad
- **B.** a pigeon
- **C.** a fish
- **D.** a sheep

6. How were operating areas first sterilized?

A. mopping the floor

B. pumping a chemical mist into the air

C. wiping down surfaces

D. airing out the area

7. Where was the oldest know medical textbook written?

A. Argentina

B. New Zealand

C. China

D. Scotland

8. Louis Pasteur was the first person to discover that organisms, some harmful, lived in the _____.

A. ocean

B. blood

C. hair

D. air

Answers

1. (B) The operation was performed by Drs. Lillehei and Lewis in Minnesota. The patient was a five-year-old girl.

2. (A) In 1796, Edward Jenner used a similar illness that occurs in cows, called "cowpox," to develop the world's first vaccine.

3. (A) Findings in Egyptian ruins show that a woman named Merit Ptah in 2700 B.C. was given the title "chief physician."

4. (C) In 1895, Wilhelm Conrad Röntgen took an X-ray of his wife's hand. Along with the bones in her hand, her wedding ring was also visible.

5. (D) Her name was Dolly and she was born in 1996. She gave birth to six lambs during her lifetime.

6. (B) Joseph Lister was the first to use a chemical solution this way. A liquid similar to his original recipe was eventually sold under his name.

7. (C) It was called *Shang Han Lun*, which means "Treatise (or discussion) on Cold Damage Disorders" in English.

8. (D) He also developed pasteurization, a process that kills harmful germs in things like milk and juice through very high temperatures.

Sports Mania

Q: What did athlete Charles Cooper accomplish in 1950?

A: He was the first African-American basketball player to be drafted into the NBA. He was tapped by the Boston Celtics.

Q: Where was the first officially recognized professional football game played?

A: Latrobe, Pennsylvania, on August 31, 1845

Q: Which two baseball players scored the same number of runs in their illustrious careers?

A: Babe Ruth and Hank Aaron

Q: Who was the first baseball player to earn $1 million a year?

A: Nolan Ryan, with the Houston Astros, in 1980.

Q: Who was the first pro hockey player to score 50 goals in one season?

A: Maurice Richard, during the 1944-1945 season (That feat was not matched until Bobby Hull did it in 1961-1962.)

Q: How long and wide is a football field?

A: It is 120 yards long and 160 feet wide.

Q: What year did girls start playing on Little League baseball teams?

A: 1974

Q: When was the first baseball game played using rules organized by Alexander Cartwright?

A: June 19, 1846, in Hoboken, New Jersey

Q: What do whale-skin eating, ear weight lifting, and seal hopping all have in common?

A: They are all events at the annual Eskimo-Indian Olympics.

Are You a Sports Fanatic?

Are you a sport lover? To find out if you're a sports fanatic, read each statement, then put a check under "True" or "False." When you're done, go to the end of the quiz to see your results!

	TRUE	FALSE
1. I have more than five sports trophies in my room.	○	○
2. I can calculate an ERA.	○	○
3. Gym is my favorite subject.	○	○
4. I prefer my football to a guitar.	○	○
5. I spend more time on a field than I do anywhere else.	○	○
6. I know who Michael Jordan is.	○	○
7. I love wearing a uniform.	○	○

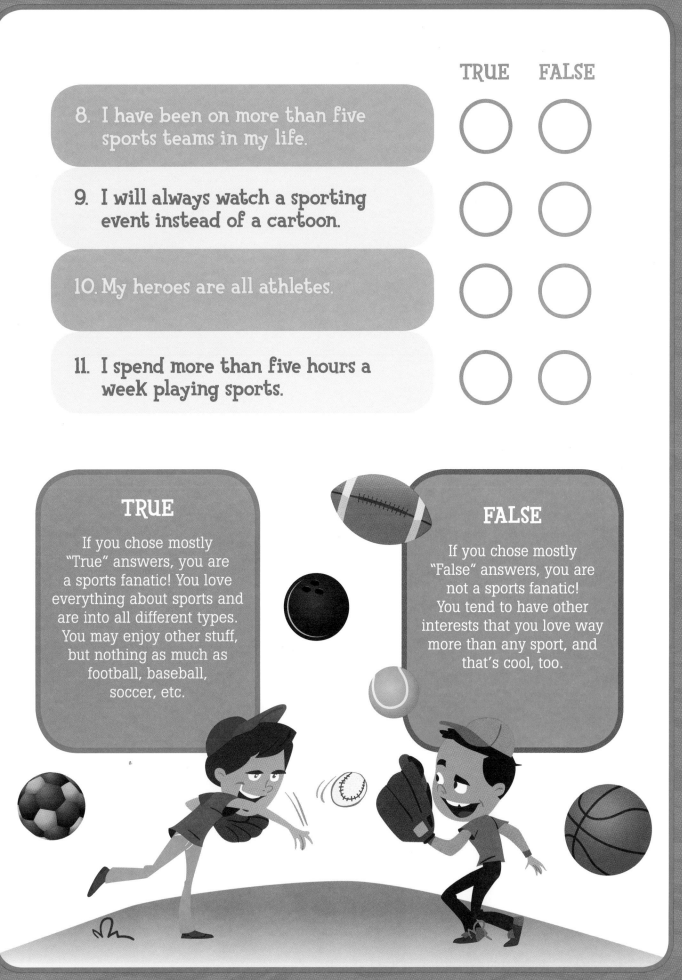

	TRUE	FALSE
8. I have been on more than five sports teams in my life.	◯	◯
9. I will always watch a sporting event instead of a cartoon.	◯	◯
10. My heroes are all athletes.	◯	◯
11. I spend more than five hours a week playing sports.	◯	◯

TRUE

If you chose mostly "True" answers, you are a sports fanatic! You love everything about sports and are into all different types. You may enjoy other stuff, but nothing as much as football, baseball, soccer, etc.

FALSE

If you chose mostly "False" answers, you are not a sports fanatic! You tend to have other interests that you love way more than any sport, and that's cool, too.

Let's Eat!

Test your knowledge of trivia relating to food with this multiple-choice quiz. Read each question and see if you can select the correct answer.

1. What is a group of bananas called?

A. finger

B. hand

C. cluster

D. groupling

2. Which fully-ripened fruit will bounce when dropped?

A. blueberry

B. cranberry

C. strawberry

D. grape

3. Which do Americans eat about 150 million of on the Fourth of July?

A. hot dogs

B. hamburgers

C. ears of corn

D. pieces of pie

4. How did the food "hamburger" get its name?

- **A.** it contains ham
- **B.** it originated in Hamburg, Germany
- **C.** it is popular in the Hamptons in New York
- **D.** it was named after Ham, the son of Noah

5. Which is the most popular pizza topping in the U.S.?

- **A.** peppers
- **B.** olives
- **C.** pepperoni
- **D.** sausage

6. Which is the most popular pizza topping in Brazil?

- **A.** pineapple
- **B.** peas
- **C.** strawberry
- **D.** banana

7. Which is considered the first puffed breakfast cereal in colonial America?

- **A.** puffed rice
- **B.** puffed wheat
- **C.** popcorn
- **D.** puffed corn

Answers

1. (B)	3. (A)	5. (C)	7. (C)
2. (B)	4. (B)	6. (B)	

FRUIT FACTS VS. FRUIT FALLACIES

Fruits are tasty and nutritious, but how much do you really know about these natural foods? Take this quiz to learn more about these sweet treats!

	TRUE	FALSE
1. Lemons contain more sugar than strawberries.	◯	◯
2. A few kinds of fruit grow their seeds on the outside.	◯	◯
3. Tomatoes, eggplants, and olives are all considered fruit.	◯	◯
4. Grapes grow in small, neat bunches.	◯	◯
5. Bananas are always yellow.	◯	◯
6. You burn more calories eating celery than you gain by eating it.	◯	◯

	TRUE	FALSE

7. Dark blueberries are usually not good to eat.

8. Peach juice is considered to be a great moisturizer and is sometimes used in cosmetics.

9. Pits–like those found in cherries or peaches–don't have any use.

10. Apples should always be peeled.

Answers

1. True.

2. False. Strawberries are the only fruit known to grow seeds this way.

3. True.

4. False. Grapes grow in large clusters of approximately 15 to 300 grapes.

5. False. There are over 100 types of bananas. They come in a variety of colors, including green, brown, and red.

6. True.

7. False. The darker a blueberry's color, the sweeter it will taste.

8. True.

9. False. Though we can't eat them, pits are the fruit's seeds. Without them, we wouldn't have a lot of fruit!

10. False. Apple peels contain important things like fiber and antioxidants (but it's okay if you don't like how the peel tastes!).

Know Your Historical Firsts

Someone had to do it first! Test your knowledge of some of the world's most important "firsts" with this multiple–choice quiz!

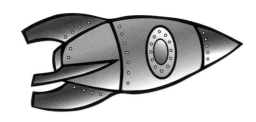

1. Sally Ride was the first American woman to enter _____.

    A. a marathon

    B. a private university

    C. a presidential race

    D. space

2. Chuck Yeager was the first person to travel faster than the speed of sound in 1947. In what vehicle did he accomplish this?

    A. a rocket-powered car

    B. a plane

    C. a spacecraft

    D. a submarine

3. Edmund Hillary is credited as being the first person to climb what massive world wonder?

    A. Mount Everest

    B. Mount Rushmore

    C. The Amazon River

    D. The Grand Canyon

4. In 1927, Charles A. Lindbergh became the first person to pilot a nonstop flight across the Atlantic. How long did it take him?

    A. 3 weeks

    B. 3 days

    C. 3 months

    D. 3 hours

5. In 1871, Ezra Sutton was the first person to ever hit a home run in a professional baseball game. Which team did he play against?

A. The Chicago White Sox

B. The Chicago White Stockings

C The Cincinnati Reds

D. The Boston Red Sox

6. Bertha Benz was the first person to drive a car over a significant distance. What was her goal?

A. to see the countryside

B. to bring her sons to school

C. to race someone on horseback

D. to prove that the automobile could be a successful product

7. The first mobile phone was developed in 1973. Weighing in at over two pounds, what nickname was the phone given?

A. the brick

B. the button

C. the bell

D. the behemoth

1. (D) Ride was also the youngest American to enter orbit.

2. (B) Yeager was asked to pilot an experimental plane, and the feat was considered highly dangerous.

3. (A) Sir Hillary was accompanied by Tenzing Norgay, a skilled Nepali mountaineer.

4. (C) Lindbergh made the journey in his plane, The Spirit of St. Louis.

5. (B) Sutton himself played for the Cleveland Forest Citys—neither team exists today.

6. (D) Benz was married to Karl Benz, inventor of the modern car and founder of the Mercedes-Benz auto company.

7. (A) The very first models of "the brick" took 10 hours to fully charge!

What Sort of Crafting Is Best for You?

Crafts help us explore our creative sides! There are tons of different activities in the crafting world—take this quiz to see if you'd like trying out a few!

1. How do you feel about visiting an art museum?
- **A.** Love it! I could walk around a museum for hours.
- **B.** Hmm . . . aren't museums full of old paintings?
- **C.** Museums are some of my favorite places. I tend to stick to the modern art.

2. What is your favorite type of book?
- **A.** Historical fiction
- **B.** I really like magazines.
- **C.** A well-constructed storybook

3. How do you go about building a sandcastle?
- **A.** With lots of orderly sections
- **B.** By mixing together all sorts of shapes
- **C.** I keep it simple and balanced.

4. You earn some extra money over the summer. Where do you spend it?
- **A.** At the print store on new photo paper
- **B.** At a bookstore, picking up some fashion magazines
- **C.** At the art supply store on paint and brushes

5. When you shop, how do you approach a store?
- **A.** I work through each section in order.
- **B.** I skip around and browse.
- **C.** I take a peek around until I see what I'm interested in.

Mostly A's

Try Scrapbooking

You are an expert collector! You may have a lot of stuff, but it's organized and neat. Your interest in the past will come in handy when digging up old photos to put in a scrapbook.

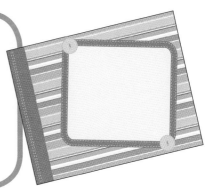

Mostly B's

Try Making a Collage

Collages allow you to make a statement, and you don't always have to be neat and tidy. Old magazines, newspapers, and even your own photos can make great resources for finding that perfect image.

Mostly C's

Fine Art and Design

Need some new art for your room? Skip the mall and create your own wall art! You have a sharp eye for design and your idea of crafting isn't limited to one thing. Let the world around you be your inspiration.

PART OF THE TEAM

Team sports are fun for everyone! Look at the clues about these awesome pastimes and see if you can fill in the blanks.

1. In American football, the offense tries to bring the ball into the opposing team's end _____. If they do this, they receive a _____ —it's worth six points.

2. Basketball players move the ball down the _____ by dribbling, or bouncing it. If they don't dribble, they are said to be _____ and will receive a penalty.

3. A _____ _____ is when a baseball player hits a ball beyond the field of play. Each baseball game is made up of nine _____.

4. Opposing volleyball teams stand on either side of a large _____. Volleyball can be played indoors or on a _____. A volleyball game begins with a _____, or when a player initially hits the ball to the other side.

5. Most professional hockey is played on _____. Players aim to move the puck with their _____. The _____ wears a protective face mask to guard against a hard-hit puck.

6. Soccer can be played on real grass or artificial _____. Players are not allowed to use their _____ while in the field's boundaries. Tight matches sometimes result in _____ shootouts where the teams take turns trying to score on each other's _____.

7. Lacrosse was first played by the Native Americans—they used long sticks and a _____ ball, just as with _____ lacrosse. Lacrosse players wear heavy _____ on their shoulders and chests. Thick _____ protect their hands from the _____ of opposing players.

8. Rugby is a full _____ sport because it is so rough and tumble. Players traditionally wear _____ with collars. Players scramble for a _____, and can be _____ for play that is too rough.

Amazing Animals

Test your knowledge of animals and their behaviors with this multiple-choice quiz. Read each question and see if you can select the correct answer.

1. A skunk belongs to the mustelidae family of animals and gives off a strong odor when disturbed. Which of these other animals is part of the same family and also gives off a strong odor?

   A. rat
   B. otter

   C. pig
   D. hamster

2. Animals that are active at night are called nocturnal; animals active by day are diurnal. What are animals that are active at twilight called?

   A. twiurnal
   B. biurnal

   C. trepscular
   D. crepuscular

3. What gives the bald eagle its name?

   A. it's bald
   B. it looks bald

   C. it loses its feathers as it ages
   D. it has a shiny crown

4. What happens to a cricket as the temperature rises?

   A. its chirp becomes slower
   B. it burrows underground

   C. its chirp becomes faster
   D. it sleeps

5. Which body part does a turtle not have?

    A. teeth   **C.** eyelids

    B. tongue   **D.** claws

6. Which animal is the largest land animal on the planet?

    A. hippopotamus   **C.** elephant

    B. rhinoceros   **D.** giraffe

7. Which is the most popular breed of pet bird in the U.S.?

    A. parrot   **C.** finch

    B. cockatiel   **D.** canary

Answers

1. (B)	3. (B)	5. (A)	7. (B)
2. (D)	4. (C)	6. (C)	

Creature Trivia

Test your animal knowledge by reading the questions and taking a guess at the answers!

Q: Are all lobsters red?

A: Only those that have been cooked in hot water. In nature, lobsters are many colors, including blue, gray, greenish-brown, and yellow—but never red.

Q: At what age does a filly become a mare?

A: Four years

Q: What is a Gila monster?

A: A type of lizard (pronounced HEE-luh) It is one of only two lizard species that are poisonous. The other is the Mexican bearded lizard.

Q: What is a group of kangaroos called?

A: A troop (other collective nouns for kangaroos: "herd" and "mob")

Q: In which direction does a fly take off from a horizontal surface?

A: Upward and backward (Now you know which way to aim the flyswatter!)

Q: What type of whale has a head that is 20 feet long, 10 feet high, and 7 feet wide?

A: The sperm whale

Q: How many different species of penguin are there?

A: 17

Q: How many living species of bears are there?

A: Eight: the Asiatic black bear, the American black bear, the brown bear, the giant panda, the polar bear, the sloth bear, the spectacled bear, and the sun bear

Q: What type of snake weighs more than any other?

A: The anaconda (It can weigh more than 1,100 pounds.)

What Kind of Tasty Beverage Should You Drink?

Looking for something to sip? Your personality can determine what sort of drink you'd like best! Take this quiz to find out.

1. Pick your favorite outfit:
- **A.** A swimsuit, or a tank top and some shorts
- **B.** A heavy cardigan, some gloves, and a scarf
- **C.** Something comfortable and easy to move around in

2. Do you like ice in a drink?
- **A.** It's essential
- **B.** No, thanks
- **C.** Eh, I could take it or leave it

3. What's your favorite thing to drink from?
- **A.** A large tumbler with lots of ice
- **B.** A nice, big mug
- **C.** A bottle or thermos

4. Do you like to play in the snow?
- **A.** Not really.
- **B.** Of course!
- **C.** I like to snowboard and sled!

5. Do you like a bubbly drink?
- **A.** Sure!
- **B.** Not so much.
- **C.** Only sometimes.

Mostly A's

A Cool Treat

You're all about relaxing and cooling off! Slushies, smoothies, sodas, and shakes—as long as it's cool and sweet—it is your thing! Try making ice cubes out of your favorite juice and add them to a glass of something tasty!

Mostly B's

A Warming Concoction

You like to be active, no matter what the season. Hot cocoa and some teas are just right for you! They help you relax after a long day, and you won't be able to get enough of the warm feeling in your tummy!

Mostly C's

Juice, Sports Drinks, or Plain Old Water

Drinking a glass of water is just the thing you need in your busy, active life! Maybe you're an athlete, or maybe you just like to keep it simple, but plain juices and water are your "cup of tea!"

A Little Bit of Everything

Test your knowledge of random trivia with this multiple-choice quiz. Read each question and see if you can select the correct answer.

1. Which is the horseshoe a symbol of?

A. wealth

B. horseback-riding ability

C. luck

D. marriage

2. Before making computer games, which did Nintendo manufacture?

A. playing cards

B. board games

C. dominoes

D. televisions

3. Which place has the largest collection of baseball cards?

A. The National Baseball Hall of Fame, Cooperstown, New York

B. The Metropolitan Museum of Art, New York City, New York

C. The Smithsonian Institution, Washington, D.C.

D. The Virginia Sports Hall of Fame and Museum, Portsmouth, Virginia

4. What color is the exterior of the black box that records flight data on commercial airplanes?

A. green

B. black

C. red

D. orange

5. To get one ounce of royal–purple dye for Cleopatra's clothes, 20,000 of which of the following had to be soaked for ten days?

A. butterfly wings
C. grapes
B. snails
D. irises

6. How are most cars in Japan sold?

A. television advertisements
C. radio advertisements
B. newspaper advertisements
D. door-to-door salespeople

7. Which is the world's tallest monument?

A. The Eiffel Tower, Paris, France
C. The Statue of Liberty, New York, New York
B. The Gateway Arch, St. Louis, Missouri
D. The Taj Mahal, Agra, India

8. What was the original name of the Rose Bowl Parade?

A. Parade of Flowers
C. Rose Petal Parade
B. Battle of Flowers
D. Coming Up Roses Parade

Answers

| 1. (C) | 3. (B) | 5. (B) | 7. (B) |
| 2. (A) | 4. (D) | 6. (D) | 8. (B) |

Famous Heroes

Being a hero takes bravery and a kind heart. Take this quiz about famous heroes from around the world—read each clue and see if you can name the hero!

Anne Frank • **Geronimo**
• **George Washington** • **Mahatma Gandhi**
• **Martin Luther King, Jr.** • **Nelson Mandela**
• **Rosa Parks** • **Sally Ride**
• **Susan B. Anthony** • **Theodore Roosevelt**

1. I am an American civil rights pioneer, and in 1963 I led the March on Washington where I delivered one of the most famous speeches of all time. **Who am I?**

2. I am most famous for the diary I kept while in hiding during World War II. It serves as a reminder of bravery in the face of oppression. **Who am I?**

3. I am a hero belonging to the Apache tribe in North America. I fiercely defended my home and family against those who wanted to take our land. **Who am I?**

4. I am a strong believer in creating change through nonviolent protests. I dedicated my life to uniting India, and to ending the unfair treatment of India by Great Britain. **Who am I?**

5. Legend has it that I got my nickname from refusing to shoot a bear while hunting. As president, I was a big supporter of conservation and the creation of national parks. **Who am I?**

_____

6. I am a military genius who fought hard against the redcoats in the American Revolution. My teeth were made from hippopotamus ivory, not wood. **Who am I?**

_____

7. I was the first American woman in space, and also a professor of physics. In my down time, I wrote children's books. **Who am I?**

_____

8. I was a main leader of the women's suffrage movement, which was an effort to give women the right to vote. Later, my face appeared on an American dollar coin. **Who am I?**

_____

9. In 1955, I refused to give up my bus seat to a white person, even though at that time African Americans were expected to go without basic civil rights. That moment sparked a citywide bus boycott and was a key moment in the fight for civil rights. **Who am I?**

_____

10. I served as South Africa's first fairly elected president. I fought hard against apartheid, a system of laws designed to oppress black people in South Africa, and was jailed for doing so. **Who am I?**

_____

ANSWERS

What Type of *Pet* Is Best For You?

Are you a first-time pet owner? Thinking about adopting a pet but not sure what kind will fit best into your life? This quiz will help you make a decision!

Dog • Cat • Reptile or Fish

1. When you're in class, how do you take notes?
- **A.** I write everything down!
- **B.** I focus in on the important bits.
- **C.** I jot down some quick notes to review later.

2. What's your favorite board game?
- **A.** I'm not a fan of board games . . .
- **B.** Chess or checkers
- **C.** Chutes and Ladders, or Candyland

3. How do you feel about group projects?
- **A.** I love them—so much fun!
- **B.** They're fine as long as everyone works together.
- **C.** Hmm, I don't really have an opinion.

4. How would you describe your group of friends?
- **A.** Big, and everyone is pretty close.
- **B.** I have a few best friends that I'd be lost without.
- **C.** Pretty big, and I have one or two really close friends.

5. It's your friend's birthday. How do you go about getting them a present?
- **A.** I go shopping and get something I know they'll like.
- **B.** I make a list and then drop hints to figure out what they want.
- **C.** I ask my friend exactly what they want.

Mostly A's
Dog

You're an active, social person, and a dog or puppy would definitely suit your personality. You're up to the physical challenge that a new dog brings, and, like a puppy, you rarely run out of energy!

Mostly B's
Cat

Cats are independent, sometimes shy creatures, but that doesn't mean that they don't have an energetic side! You'll appreciate the need for a cat to be off on its own at times, but you'll be ready to play when it feels frisky.

Mostly C's
A Reptile or Fish

These creatures are totally straightforward. You'll know when they need to eat, when they're sick, and when they don't require much attention. You'll love taking care of these simple little creatures, and they'll love the care and effort you put into creating their new home!

Prehistoric Pop Quiz

Dinosaurs lived long, long ago and, just like animals today, there were many different species of dinosaur. Take this quiz to test your knowledge of these prehistoric reptiles.

1. What does the word "dinosaur" translate to in Greek?

A. huge reptile

B. big feet

C. ancient ones

D. terrible lizard

2. The largest of the dinosaurs ate _____.

A. plants

B. meat

C. plants and other animals

D. everything in sight

3. What is closest in size to the brain of a stegosaurus?

A. a pea

B. a walnut

C. an orange

D. a soccer ball

4. What killed the dinosaurs?

A. a huge meteor

B. a volcanic eruption

C. a drastic temperature change

D. no one knows

5. Which of the following IS a dinosaur?

A. Gila monster

B. Pteranodon

C. Allosaurus

D. Plesiosaur

6. About how fast could Tyrannosaurus rex run?

A. 10 miles per hour   **C.** 40 miles per hour

B. 25 miles per hour   **D.** 50 miles per hour

7. Which is a similarity between dinosaurs and modern birds?

A. hollow backbones   **C.** feeding habits

B. scaly skin   **D.** behavior of babies

8. How long did dinosaurs live on Earth?

A. 10 million years   **C.** 100 million years

B. 50 million years   **D.** 150 million years

Answers

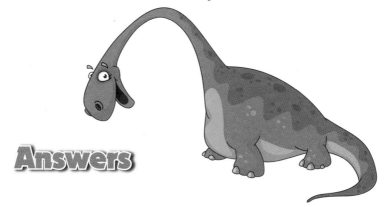

1. (D) The paleontologist Richard Owen first used the word "dinosaur" in 1842.

2. (A) The largest dinosaurs, like Brachiosaurus, were herbivorous and had long necks to eat from tall trees.

3. (B) Even though the Stegosaurus weighed almost two tons, it had one of the smallest brains (relative to size) in the dinosaur world.

4. (D) Scientists aren't sure! But A, B, and C have all been thought of as possible explanations for the dinosaurs' extinction.

5. (C) True dinosaurs lived on land. Plesiosaur was a sea reptile, and Pteranodon was a flying reptile. Gila monsters are large, modern lizards.

6. (B) Not so fast for an animal of its size. The T. rex was an awkward–moving dinosaur and needed almost half its mass in its legs to run at all.

7. (A) Birds need light, hollow bones in order to fly. Some scientists believe that birds descended from dinosaurs.

8. (D) For perspective, humans have only been alive for a few hundred-thousand years.

Fun For All Quiz

Almost everyone loves to be entertained —whether it's watching a movie, reading a book, or playing a game. Test your knowledge of trivia relating to entertainment with this multiple-choice quiz. Read each question and see if you can select the correct answer.

1. Which film won the first Academy Award for best picture in 1929?

    A. *The Bridge of San Luis Rey*   **C.** *Dance Hall*

    B. *Wings*   **D.** *Broadway*

2. What toy was originally called Atomic Building Bricks when it was created in 1949?

    A. Tinker Toys   **C.** Lincoln Logs

    B. Pick–Up Sticks   **D.** Legos

3. What is the longest-running TV show on network television?

    A. *The Simpsons*   **C.** *Family Guy*

    B. *Meet the Press*   **D.** *Nightly News*

4. Who was the first performer to win an Oscar®, Emmy®, Tony®, and Grammy®?

    A. Barbra Streisand   **C.** Beyoncé

    B. Taylor Swift   **D.** Fergie

5. What is the name of the dog owned by the Grinch in *The Grinch Who Stole Christmas*?

A. Fido

C. Lucifer

B. Max

D. Rover

6. What was the first–ever Hollywood movie to be shown on network TV in 1955?

A. *The Sound of Music*

C. *Rebel Without a Cause*

B. *The Wizard of Oz*

D. *Some Like It Hot*

7. Which fictional detective lived at 221B Baker Street, London, England?

A. Sherlock Holmes

C. Hercule Poirot

B. Jane Marple

D. Harriet the Spy

8. What did Bela Lugosi, famous for playing Count Dracula, request he be buried wearing?

A. fangs

C. fake blood

B. black cape

D. black wig

Answers

1. (B)	3. (B)	5. (C)	7. (A)
2. (D)	4. (A)	6. (B)	8. (B)

Scientifically Correct

Test your science knowledge by reading the questions and taking a guess at the answers!

Q: How fast does a lightning bolt travel?

A: About 60,000 miles per second

Q: What did Johann Wilhelm Ritter discover in 1801?

A: Ultraviolet light—part of the color spectrum of the light that is invisible to the human eye

Q: Who was Peking man?

A: An early ancestor of humans (Our knowledge of him is based on fossilized bones, 130,000 to 900,000 years old, that were found in China near Beijing (once known as Peking). Peking man had a thick skull and brow, with a small forehead and large jaw.)

Q: What country uses more industrial robots than any other?

A: Japan (It uses more than half of the world total.)

Q: Who invented the electric battery?

A: Alessandro Volta (1745–1827), an Italian physicist

Q: Who was the first person to use a parachute—and survive?

A: Leonardo da Vinci came up with the idea in 1483. However, no one succeeded in parachuting from a great height until André-Jacques Garnerin. In 1797, he proved his parachute's worth by jumping from a hot-air balloon 3,000 feet up—and making it safely to the ground.

Q: The first public electric railway opened in 1881. Where?

A: In Germany (It was an electric tramway that ran from Lichterfelde, near Berlin, to a cadet academy—a distance of about 1.7 miles.)

Q: Who is considered the father of modern chemistry?

A: Antoine-Laurent Lavoisier (1743–1794) Among his many contributions was his explanation of combustion—the chemical process that creates fire—and oxygen's role in it. He was also the first to explain how animals and plants use oxygen, and why they need it to survive.

Are You a Good Best Friend?

Are you a good friend? Read each statement, and then put a check under "Like Me" or "Not Like Me." When you're done, go to the end of the quiz to find out if you're best friend material.

LIKE ME | NOT LIKE ME

1. I know my best friend's birthday–and make it a point to make her a gift.

2. When we're in school, I try to save her a seat.

3. I'm always around to act as a sounding board.

4. I'd never tell her crush what she says about him.

5. When my mom bakes something yummy, I bring some extras to share.

6. We have similar interests–be it hobbies or boys.

7. At least once a week, we make plans to hang out.

8. If we have a class together, we make perfect study buddies.

9. I'm never mean to her.

10. She knows that she can trust me with top-secret info.

11. I've invited her over for a sleepover party.

12. People say that we're "two peas in a pod."

13. She'll only tell me what scares her.

14. We hang out so much that we even finish each other's sentences.

15. If something is ever wrong, I'm always the first one she talks to.

Tally it up!

If you chose mostly "Like Me" answers, you're a true-blue best friend! There's no replacing you. You're always around when she needs you the most. And the best part is, that you can count on her, too.

If you chose mostly "Not Like Me" answers, you need to work on your friendship skills! Sometimes you flake or don't agree with your friend. It sounds like the two of you need to work on your communication skills.

That's Entertainment!

Almost everyone loves to be entertained—whether it's watching a movie, reading a book, or playing a game. Test your knowledge of trivia relating to entertainment with this multiple-choice quiz. Read each question and see if you can select the correct answer.

1. Why did filmmakers have to slow the film of Bruce Lee movies?

A. to show his moves in slow motion

B. he was too fast to be seen

C. to time the film to music

D. to switch in a stand-in actor

2. Who composed the children's song "Twinkle, Twinkle, Little Star" when he was just five years old?

A. Chopin

B. Beethoven

C. Mozart

D. Elvis Presley

3. What was Sleeping Beauty's real name?

A. Aurora

B. Anastasia

C. Ariel

D. Antoinette

4. What is the first thing Winnie the Pooh says each morning?

A. "I'm rumbly in my tummy."

B. "What's for breakfast?"

C. "Where's my honey?"

D. "Oh, bother."

5. Where was the first screening of a giant screen IMAX film?

    A. America   **C.** Japan

    B. Europe   **D.** China

6. Which American play was based on Shakespeare's *Romeo and Juliet*?

    A. West Side Story   **C.** Guys and Dolls

    B. Grease   **D.** South Pacific

7. The average American watches how many hours of television a month?

    A. 60 hours   **C.** 100 hours

    B. 10 hours   **D.** 120 hours

8. Which was inducted into the National Toy Hall of Fame in Rochester, NY?

    A. yo-yo   **C.** jigsaw puzzle

    B. pogo stick   **D.** badminton set

Answers

1. (B)	3. (A)	5. (C)	7. (D)
2. (C)	4. (B)	6. (A)	8. (C)

How Do You Deal With Surprises?

Do you always do things the same way, or do you like to look for new adventures? Take this quiz then add up your points to figure out how well you deal with surprises.

Fear • Caution • Enthusiasm

1. **You and your best friend always have lunch together on Fridays. One Friday, your bud brings the new girl in school along with her. You—**
   A. Be polite, but use some secret signals to let your pal know how upset you are that she brought along an intruder. (4)
   B. Pretend the new girl isn't there and just talk to your bud. (2)
   C. Help the new girl feel welcome by showing her the best places in town to eat. (6)

2. **Your parents said that your friend could color your hair with her all-natural hair dye. But instead of blonde, it turned out bright orange! You—**
   A. Stay home from school until you can change the color. (2)
   B. Wear a sign that says: "My best friend did this to me!" (4)
   C. Pick out an outfit that goes with orange, and act like you planned the whole thing. (6)

3. **Your parents take you to your favorite Chinese restaurant. You order your usual, but the waiter brings you some strange dish that you never heard of. You—**
   A. Dig in! here's a chance to try a dish that you probably never would have ordered. (6)
   B. Try to swap dishes with one of your parents. (2)
   C. Send it back and watch everybody eat until your food arrives. (4)

4. **A family from another country moves in next door. They have a girl your age. You—**
   A. Take her some brownies and introduce yourself. Then make a date to visit again, so she can fix you some cool snack food from her country. (6)
   B. Ignore her, since you probably have nothing in common. (4)
   C. Wait to see what she's like in school before you get friendly with her. (2)

5. **You're at the movie theater waiting in line for a movie you've been dying to see. The 7:30 showing is sold out and the next one is past your curfew. The only other movie playing now is a black-and-white movie from the 1960s. You—**
   - **A.** Forget the movies. Instead, go to the ice-cream shop next door and have a big ice-cream sundae with your movie money. (4)
   - **B.** Call your parents and ask them to come get you immediately. There's no way you're going to sit through some movie that's over 50 years old. (4)
   - **C.** Decide to give the old movie a try since you're already there. There must be some reason it's been around this long. (2)

Fear 10-15 points

You may be surprised to learn that the key to your score is fear. Change seems like a very scary thing to you. The next time something different or unexpected happens, try to think of it as an adventure.

Caution 16-24 points

You sometimes are too cautious and tend to worry too much about what people think of you. Trust yourself more and you'll do fine in new situations.

Enthusiasm 25-30 points

You are eager for new experiences. You like to try new things. Keep it up and you will have many excellent adventures in life!

Critter Fun Facts

Test your knowledge of animals and their behaviors with this multiple-choice quiz. Read each question and see if you can select the correct answer.

1. Which animal can spring 18 feet into the air—straight up?

- **A.** kangaroo
- **B.** cougar
- **C.** monkey
- **D.** jackal

2. Which primate is most closely related to the human?

- **A.** orangutan
- **B.** gorilla
- **C.** chimpanzee
- **D.** bamboo lemur

3. Which animals did President Martin Van Buren receive as a gift?

- **A.** grizzly cubs
- **B.** tiger cubs
- **C.** panda cubs
- **D.** badger cubs

4. The human eye has one lens. Which critter has 30,000 lenses?

- **A.** dragonfly
- **B.** garter snake
- **C.** honeybee
- **D.** bullfrog

5. Which dinosaur had the longest neck?

    A. Brachiosaurus   **C.** T. rex

    B. Iguanodon   **D.** Mamenchisaurus

6. Which animal does not live in the Arctic, but lives only in the Southern Hemisphere in Antarctica?

    A. hare   **C.** snowy owl

    B. penguin   **D.** fox

7. What do gelada, macaque, and proboscis have in common?

    A. they're all types of monkeys **C.** they are all nocturnal

    B. they can all fly   **D.** they are all types of birds

8. Which is the world's largest living bird?

    A. flamingo   **C.** ostritch

    B. eagle   **D.** heron

Answers

    1. (C)   3. (B)   5. (D)   7. (A)

    2. (C)   4. (A)   6. (B)   8. (C)

Worldwide Trivia

Test your worldly knowledge with this multiple-choice quiz! Read each question and see if you can select the correct answer.

1. Which U.S. state did the Dutch and Swedes settle?

A. New Jersey   **C.** New York

B. Pennsylvania   **D.** Connecticut

2. How long is the Great Wall of China?

A. 1,034 miles   **C.** 3,915 miles

B. 425 miles   **D.** 5,015 miles

3. Which is the only U.S. state to have parishes instead of counties?

A. Georgia   **C.** North Carolina

B. South Carolina   **D.** Louisiana

4. Which English landmark celebrated its 150th anniversary on May 31, 2009?

A. Stonehenge   **C.** Buckingham Palace

B. Big Ben   **D.** The London Eye

5. What does the state of Oregon grow more of than any other U.S. State?

A. apple trees

B. corn

C. Christmas trees

D. potatoes

6. What is the longest river in the world?

A. Amazon River

B. Mississippi River

C. Huang He River

D. Nile River

7. Which New York landmark stands 152 feet tall?

A. The Chrysler Building

B. The Empire State Building

C. The Statue of Liberty

D. Grand Central Station

8. What is Aphrodite the Greek goddess of?

A. love & beauty

B. fame & fortune

C. speed & agility

D. strength & power

Answers

1. (A)	3. (D)	5. (C)	7. (C)
2. (C)	4. (B)	6. (D)	8. (D)

Test your sports knowledge by reading the questions and taking a guess at the answers!

Q: How many consecutive strikes does it take to bowl a perfect game?

A: 12 (a score of 300)

Q: Which kind of sporting equipment outsells baseballs, basketballs, and footballs combined?

A: Frisbees®

Q: In rodeo-competition bull riding, how long must the rider hang on?

A: Eight seconds

Q: Cy Young holds the record for most games won by a major-league pitcher: 511. What was his real name?

A: Denton True Young (Cy was short for "cyclone" because of the speed of his fastball.)

Q: In baseball, the distance between bases is 90 feet. What is the size of the first, second, and third bases?

A: 15" x 15" (and 3" deep)

Q: Which heavyweight boxing champ was once knocked out of the ring in the first round, yet came back to win the second round?

A: Jack Dempsey (against Linus Angel Firpo on September 14, 1923)

Q: What game requires the largest playing field?

A: Polo (Those ponies need a lot of room to run! A polo field is 300 yards long and 160 yards wide.)

Q: A feathery was an item used in which sport in the 17th century?

A: Golf (A feathery was a golf ball made from boiled feathers that were squeezed into a stitched-leather cover.)

Q: Who was the only pro basketball player to score 100 points in a single regulation game?

A: Wilt Chamberlain on March 2, 1962, vs. the New York Knicks (Chamberlain's Philadelphia Warriors won 169–147.)

Are You Best Friend Material?

You would do absolutely anything for your best friend, right? Put yourself to the test and see how good a friend you would be in these ultra-sticky situations.

Honest Chick · Close Friend · Best Bud

1. **Your best friend has a crush—on the same guy you do! She has asked you to talk to him and find out if he likes her. What do you do?**
   - **A.** You get "uncrushed" on your sweetheart and talk to him on behalf of your best friend. (2)
   - **B.** You have a heart-to-heart with your best friend and work through the problem. (3)
   - **C.** You talk to your crush—flirt with him actually—and never mention your best friend. After all, you knew him first! (1)

2. **Your best friend has just bought a new dress for a fancy family occasion. She absolutely loves it. Problem is, you think it's ugly. What do you do?**
   - **A.** You take a deep breath, then gently tell her the truth. (3)
   - **B.** You tell her not to bother leaving the house. (1)
   - **C.** You tell her she looks stunning, so as to not hurt her feelings. (2)

3. **Your best friend has just returned your MP3 player after she borrowed it. When you turn it on, you notice something is not right. What do you do?**
   - **A.** You call your friend and ask her if something happened to it. (3)
   - **B.** You call your friend and yell at her for breaking your MP3 player. (1)
   - **C.** You don't say anything about it, but you decide never to lend her anything valuable again. (2)

4. **You're out with your family on a Friday night when you spot your best friend's boyfriend with a pretty girl you've never seen before. What do you do?**
   - **A.** You slip away from the table and call your friend. (1)
   - **B.** You call her when you get home, sad to break the bad news, but happy to provide emotional support. (3)
   - **C.** You see her the next day and don't mention a word about it so as to not hurt her feelings. (2)

5. During lunch, you overhear two girls gossiping about your best friend. You know your best friend likes these particular girls. What do you do?

   A. You stick up for your friend in front of the two girls, then don't mention a word of what happened to your friend. (2)

   B. You run back and tell your friend what the girls said about her—even if it hurts her feelings. (1)

   C. You tell your friend to stay clear of those girls because they like to talk behind a person's back. (3)

Honest Chick 5-8 points

If you scored 5 to 8 points, you're a little rough around the edges. You are usually honest with your friends, but a little insensitive. Remember that part of a healthy friendship is being kind and offering your friend support.

Close Friend 9-11 points

If you scored 9 to 11 points, you're a good friend overall. However, you sometimes sacrifice the truth for what you believe is kindness. Keep in mind that close friends are honest friends.

Best Bud 12-15 points

If you scored 12 to 15 points, you really know how to communicate with your best bud! When something is bothering you, you let her know. When she's in a tight spot, you help her out. Keep up the good work!

Foodie Trivia

Do you love to eat? Do you enjoy trying new foods? Test your knowledge of trivia relating to food with this multiple-choice quiz. Read each question and see if you can select the correct answer.

1. To which family of plants does garlic belong?

    A. tulip   **C.** peony

    B. lily   **D.** fern

2. Which fruit starts out as a lavender-colored flower?

    A. orange   **C.** coconut

    B. banana   **D.** pineapple

3. About 60 percent of all of which type of sandwich is eaten in the U.S.?

    A. bacon, lettuce, tomato   **C.** hamburger

    B. tuna salad   **D.** peanut-butter and jelly

4. Americans eat more than 100 acres of which type of food each day?

    A. french fries   **C.** hot dogs

    B. pizza   **D.** chicken nuggets

5. About 10 quarts of milk are needed to make one pound of which product?

    A. ice cream   **C.** butter

    B. cake   **D.** cream cheese

6. What was the original name of potato chips?

    A. crispies   **C.** crunchies

    B. Saratoga chips   **D.** potatoe crunches

7. About 30,000 of which item can be made from one acre of peanuts?

    A. peanut butter cups   **C.** peanut butter and jelly sandwiches

    B. peanut butter cupcakes   **D.** peanut butter ice cream

8. About 70 percent of all of which product is consumed at home?

    A. popcorn   **C.** rigatoni

    B. sushi   **D.** cereal

Answers

1. (B)	3. (C)	5. (C)	7. (C)
2. (D)	4. (B)	6. (B)	8. (A)

How Do You Get Your Exercise?

The key to sticking to an exercise routine is finding the kind of workout that you find the most fun. Take this quiz to figure out what kind of exercise may be the right one for you!

Cardio · Weights · Sports

1. How would you describe your study routine?
- **A.** I like to bring my notes to a study group—I work best with other people. (3)
- **B.** Slow and steady. I don't mind taking a while to get something right. (2)
- **C.** Alone, with music playing. Sometimes being a little distracted helps. (3)

2. It's time to relax! What are your plans?
- **A.** Spend some time trying to beat my friend's high score in our favorite video game! (2)
- **B.** Take a load off and read something I've been meaning to get to. (1)
- **C.** Round up all my friends and head out for a night at the movies. (3)

3. It's time to pick a sport in gym class. What do you pick?
- **A.** Soccer, volleyball, lacrosse, kickball…I can't make a decision! (3)
- **B.** Step aerobics or pilates—something that I can do while zoning out. (1)
- **C.** Volleyball, baseball, or anything that doesn't involve too much moving around! (2)

4. What type of movie do you like the best?
- **A.** Action movies (2)
- **B.** Sports movies (3)
- **C.** Spy movies (1)

5. How do you feel about "alone time?"
- **A.** I don't mind it all. (1)
- **B.** It's OK, everyone needs some now and then. (2)
- **C.** I hate it! (3)

Cardio 5-8 points

You like cardio! Things like running, jogging, walking, and using machines like treadmills are all great for your heart. You may prefer to work out alone, and might even benefit from the quiet time.

Weights 9-11 points

You like lifting weights! You don't mind working out around people, but being alone isn't a problem, either. You are focused on overcoming sizable goals!

Sports 12-15 points

You like team sports! You do your best when surrounded by others to push and support you. You're naturally competitive, so use this to your advantage while maintaining a healthy regimen.

Geography Quiz

Are you the person people go to when they're lost? Do you always get A's in geography class? Test your knowledge of geography with this multiple-choice quiz. Read each question and see if you can select the correct answer.

1. Where is the world's largest St. Patrick's Day parade held?

A. Dublin, Ireland

B. Boston, Massachusetts

C. Chicago, Illinois

D. New York, New York

2. Which is the largest country by land area?

A. Canada

B. Indonesia

C. Russia

D. Korea

3. Which is the official state bird of Hawaii?

A. Goose

B. Mallard duck

C. Surf scoter

D. Green heron

4. Which continent has the greatest variety of plants and animals?

A. Africa

B. North America

C. South America

D. Asia

5. How many cities in the world have a population of more than 1 million people?

    A. more than 500   **C.** more than 600

    B. more than 400   **D.** more than 800

6. Not counting the continent of Australia, which is the largest island on Earth?

    A. Sumatra   **C.** Great Britain

    B. Greenland   **D.** Madagascar

7. Where was the world's first subway system built, in 1863?

    A. London, England   **C.** Barcelona, Spain

    B. New York, New York   **D.** Stockholm, Sweden

Answers

1. (D)   3. (A)   5. (C)   7. (B)

2. (C)   4. (C)   6. (B)

This and That Quiz

Do you know a little about a lot of different things—that's called trivia! Test your knowledge of trivia with this multiple-choice quiz. Read each question and see if you can select the correct answer.

1. **Which happens in the U.S., Canada, and Britain to 1 out of every 83.4 births?**

   A. The baby has red hair.

   B. The babies are twins.

   C. The baby has one brown eye and one blue eye.

   D. The baby weighs more than 9 pounds.

2. **Which was the usual greeting when people first started using telephones?**

   A. Hello?

   B. What's up?

   C. Who's calling?

   D. Are you there?

3. **Which of the following is on display at the National Air and Space Museum in Washington, DC?**

   A. The first hot–air balloon

   B. The original model of the Starship Enterprise

   C. The first helicopter

   D. The first rocket ship launched from the U.S.

4. **What does the average person do for two hours in their sleep each night?**

   A. snore

   B. blink

   C. dream

   D. talk

5. Which president had a wallaby, bobcat, and pygmy hippopotamus as pets?

    A. James Madison   **C.** Franklin D. Roosevelt

    B. Lyndon Johnson   **D.** Calvin Coolidge

6. Who made the phrase "rock 'n' roll" popular?

    A. Elvis Presley   **C.** Disc jockey Dick Clark

    B. Disc jockey Alan Freed   **D.** Mick Jagger

7. What did pirates, among other seamen of the time, wear to prevent seasickness?

    A. bracelets   **C.** swords

    B. eye patches   **D.** earrings

8. Where does catgut—used in tennis rackets, surgery, and stringed instruments—come from?

    A. cactus   **C.** sheep

    B. cat   **D.** goats

Answers

1. (B)	3. (B)	5. (D)	7. (D)
2. (D)	4. (C)	6. (B)	8. (C)

Big Cat FACTS

"Big cats" are the wild felines of the world—lions, tigers, and leopards are all big cats! See how much you know about these fascinating creatures by taking this quiz.

TRUE   FALSE

1. The male in a pride of lions is responsible for most of the work.

2. The largest cat that can purr is the mountain lion, or cougar.

3. Each tiger's stripes are unique, and scientists use them to identify individuals.

4. All cats HATE water.

5. The cheetah is the fastest land animal in the world and can go from zero to 70 miles per hour in three seconds.

6. Black panthers evolved their dark color to hide in the jungle.

7. Leopards are excellent climbers and can drag kills multiple times their own weight high up into trees.

8. Ligers are crosses between lions and tigers. They can grow larger than either a lion or tiger.

9. Lions have the loudest roar of the big cats because of their large lungs.

10. Cheetahs are renowned scavengers.

Answers

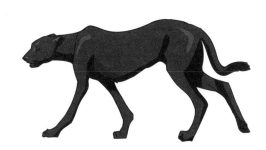

1. False. The female lions, or lionesses, are responsible for hunting and raising cubs. The male defends the pride, only on rare occasions.

2. True.

3. True.

4. False. Bengal tigers will stalk prey from water, and jaguars head to the beach to feast on nesting turtles.

5. True.

6. False. There is no such thing as a black panther. Some jaguars have a genetic trait called melanism that makes their fur black instead of spotted.

7. True.

8. True.

9. False. Lions have the loudest roar because they have the largest larynx, a structure in the throat.

10. False. Cheetahs actually refuse to scavenge and may lose their prey to scavengers like hyenas or groups of wild dogs.

How Do You Deal with the Unexpected?

How do you handle last-second plans? Read each statement, and then put a check under "Like Me" or "Not Like Me" to find out how you deal with the unexpected.

LIKE ME NOT LIKE ME

1. I get ready for school the night before— pack my lunch, get my outfit together, etc.

2. I hate horror or suspense movies!

3. Pop quiz? No big deal!

4. I blush very easily.

5. I don't mind when I'm called on in class, even if I'm focused on doodling in my notebook.

6. My friends always let me know about weekend plans way in advance.

7. I like to read books without knowing what they're about.

8. If I get an unexpected call from my crush, I will run to the phone!

9. I like to shop for whatever reason—I don't need to have a specific thing in mind.

10. The idea of a surprise party thrills me!

11. If a classmate cancels a meeting for a project, I just try to reschedule.

12. On the first day of school, if my classes aren't exactly what I picked, you can find me sorting things out in the office.

13. My soccer coach knows I'm happy playing anywhere on the field.

14. I'm an understudy for the lead role in the school play...but I really hope no one gets sick before opening night!

15. My favorite kind of party is a surprise party, of course!

Tally it up!

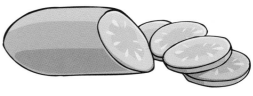

If you chose mostly "Like Me" answers, you are great at handling the unexpected! You're as cool as a cucumber. You can really roll with the punches.

If you chose mostly "Not Like Me" answers, you'd rather know about something in advance than be surprised! You're an excellent planner, but sometimes that means you get caught up in events.

Time to BOOT UP!

Can you imagine a world without computers? Take this quiz to find out how computers became such a huge part of daily life!

TRUE FALSE

1. Early computers were close to the same size they are today. ◯ ◯

2. Computers aren't just desktops or laptops—small computers are in cell phones, cars, music players, and even some toys. ◯ ◯

3. Simple computers are a fairly new invention. ◯ ◯

4. A computer's memory is located in something called a motherboard. ◯ ◯

5. A computer virus can cause loss of memory and overall damage to a computer's programs. ◯ ◯

6. The Internet was originally invented so people in different places could play the same games together. ◯ ◯

7. The first computer mouse, created in 1964 by Doug Englebart, was made of wood.

8. The circuits inside a computer are incredibly durable.

9. Most people in the world use computers and the Internet.

10. Early storage discs cost several hundred dollars. Today, you can get the same size storage device for a few dollars.

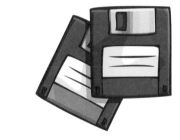

Answers

1. False. The first computers of the 1940s were often large enough to fill a room.

2. True.

3. False. The Chinese abacus is thousands of years old. It uses beads to keep track of numbers and is therefore considered a kind of computer.

4. True.

5. True.

6. False. The Internet was created by the U.S. Department of Defense as an easy way to send messages.

7. True.

8. False. Internal circuitry is sensitive and can be damaged by simple static electricity.

9. False. Many people still don't use computers. Sweden has the highest percentage of Internet users at around 75 percent.

10. True.

What Do You Know?

Do you know a little about a lot of different things—that's called trivia! Test your knowledge of trivia with this multiple-choice quiz. Read each question and see if you can select the correct answer.

1. Which U.S. state has the most roller coasters in operation?

    A. Texas   **C.** California

    B. Florida   **D.** Arizona

2. A googol is the number one followed by how many zeroes?

    A. 100   **C.** 1 million

    B. 1,000   **D.** 10,000

3. On an average weekday, two billion of which of the following things are made in the U.S.?

    A. hamburgers   **C.** pizzas

    B. telephone calls   **D.** beds

4. Which is one of the oldest known playthings?

    A. jumprope   **C.** bicycle

    B. skateboard   **D.** doll

5. What is the average number of bunnies a cottontail rabbit has per year?

    A. 12   **C.** 100

    B. 24   **D.** 84

6. Which is the best-selling musical instrument in the world?

    A. guitar   **C.** harmonica

    B. violin   **D.** flute

7. Which was the first toy ever to be advertised on network television in 1952?

    A. Mr. Potato Head   **C.** G.I. Joe

    B. Barbie   **D.** Radio Flyer wagon

8. What was the Leaning Tower of Pisa built to serve as?

    A. radio tower   **C.** bell tower

    B. clock tower   **D.** cooking tower

Answers

1. (C)	3. (B)	5. (D)	7. (A)
2. (A)	4. (D)	6. (C)	8. (C)

What Kind of Wild Cat Are You Most Like?

Lion · Tiger · Jaguar

1. How would you describe your group of friends?
- **A.** A large group of people with all different sorts of personalities and interests (1)
- **B.** On the small side and mostly interested in the same things (2)
- **C.** High-energy and extremely motivated (3)

2. What's your favorite thing to do when you feel like being lazy?
- **A.** Soak up some sun! (3)
- **B.** Go for a relaxing swim. (2)
- **C.** Nap! (1)

3. Do you exercise?
- **A.** Sure, it's part of staying in shape. (2)
- **B.** Only when I have to… (1)
- **C.** It's one of my favorite things to do! (3)

4. Which class office would you most likely run for?
- **A.** President, obviously! (1)
- **B.** Vice president or treasurer—I don't want too much of the spotlight. (2)
- **C.** Events coordinator—I like being behind the scenes. (3)

5. When are you most active or motivated?
- **A.** In the morning and for most of the afternoon. (3)
- **B.** From late afternoon to the early evening. (2)
- **C.** At night. (1)

6. What do you like most about yourself?
- **A.** My focus and strength—once I commit to something, I make sure it gets done! (2)
- **B.** My courage and ability to organize other people. (1)
- **C.** My energy and willingness to work on many different things at once. (3)

Lion 6-9 points

You are most like a lion! You are real leadership material and have a big network of friends and people who look up to you. Nothing phases you!

Tiger 10-14 points

You are most like a tiger! You always get the job done, even if you're working alone. Never underestimate your ability to achieve a goal.

Jaguar 15-18 points

You are most like a jaguar! You have so much energy, both physically and when it comes to doing all sorts of things at once. You are unstoppable!

Animals Everywhere!

Test your knowledge of animals and their behaviors with this multiple-choice quiz. Read each question and see if you can select the correct answer.

1. Which bird must eat 100 percent of its body weight every day?

    A. wild turkey   **C.** nightjar

    B. ruby-throated hummingbird   **D.** yellow-belly finch

2. How many eggs does the average hen lay per week?

    A. 10   **C.** 3

    B. 7   **D.** 5

3. Which creatures are responsible for the most human deaths each year?

    A. rattlesnakes   **C.** scorpions

    B. bees and wasps   **D.** red ants

4. Which is the largest fish in the ocean?

    A. yellowfin tuna   **C.** whale shark

    B. marlin   **D.** oarfish

5. Which endangered species has fewer than 1,000 members left in the wild?

A. blue whale
B. leopard

C. numbat
D. giant panda

6. Which breed of dog is most commonly used in search-and-rescue operations?

A. Labrador retriever
B. German shepherd

C. husky
D. greyhound

7. Which of the following characteristics applies to bats?

A. they are blind
B. they are colorblind

C. they have night blindness
D. they cannot see in daylight

8. In 1964, Smokey the Bear became so popular he was given which of the following?

A. his own address
B. his own telephone number

C. his own television show
D. his own zip code

Answers

| 1. (B) | 3. (B) | 5. (D) | 7. (B) |
| 2. (D) | 4. (C) | 6. (B) | 8. (B) |

EGYPTIAN MUMMIES

Mummies are more than just spooky Halloween monsters! Take this quiz to learn about some of the world's most famous mummies—Egyptian mummies.

1. Why did ancient Egyptians leave the heart inside their mummies?

A. They thought people needed a heart to enter the afterlife.

B. They believed the heart was the center of thought and emotion.

C. They thought the heart would ward off evil spirits.

D. The heart is small and was often forgotten by mummy makers.

2. What important ingredient did the Egyptians use during mummification?

A. oil

B. water

C. sand

D. salt

3. Mummified pharaohs were often buried with what?

A. nets

B. servants

C. food

D. all of the above

4. In the late 1800s, what was the biggest threat to a mummy's tomb?

A. robbers

B. weather

C. mice and bugs

D. demolition

5. What is "mummiya"?

A. a type of glue that held a mummy's wrapping together

B. a place with a lot of mummies

C. a powder made from ground–up mummies

D. the name of a famous mummy family

6. What kind of scientist is responsible for uncovering mummies and learning from them?

A. archeologist   C. geologist

B. paleontologist   D. historian

7. What is the name of the Egyptian god of mummification?

A. Osiris   C. Isis

B. Anubis   D. Zeus

8. What is the secret behind "King Tut's Curse"?

A. a mosquito bite   C. a wild imagination

B. a group of pranksters   D. a phantom

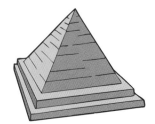

Answers

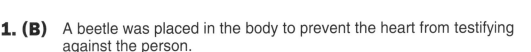

1. (B) A beetle was placed in the body to prevent the heart from testifying against the person.

2. (D) The salt was called natron and was actually made up of a few varieties of naturally occurring salt.

3. (D) Ancient Egyptians believed that people needed supplies for the afterlife, so they were entombed with all that they used in real life.

4. (A) People would often break into tombs to steal the valuable jewelry inside. The Egyptian government eventually made it illegal to steal artifacts.

5. (C) In Europe, people believed mummiya could cure illness. Mummiya is also the Arabic word for a black, tar-like substance that people thought appeared on mummies.

6. (A) People can also specialize in the study of ancient Egypt. They are called Egyptologists.

7. (B) Lots of Egyptian gods and goddesses had human bodies and animal heads. Anubis had the head of a jackal.

8. (A) Lord Carnavron died from pneumonia induced by a mosquito bite shortly after opening King Tut's tomb. From then on, people believed the tomb to be cursed.

Q: What popular game was originally called mintonette?

A: Volleyball

Q: A tennis player scoring for the first time in a match earns how many points?

A: 15

Q: How many leather panels are on a regulation soccer ball?

A: 32

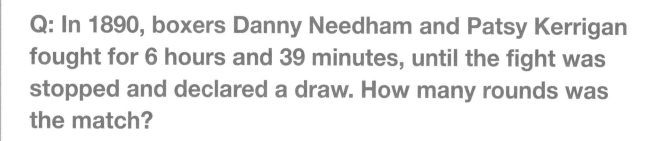

Q: In 1890, boxers Danny Needham and Patsy Kerrigan fought for 6 hours and 39 minutes, until the fight was stopped and declared a draw. How many rounds was the match?

A: 100

Q: "Hang ten" is an expression used in which sport?

A: Surfing (from hanging 10 toes off the edge of a surfboard)

Q: On July 1947, Larry Doby became the first African-American player in baseball's American League when he joined what team?

A: The Cleveland Indians

Q: How many batters does a pitcher face in a perfect game—with no runs, hits, errors, walks, or batters hit?

A: 27

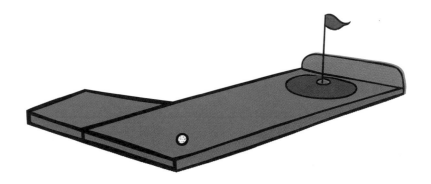

Q: Where were the first outdoor miniature-golf courses built?

A: On New York City rooftops in 1926

Q: When an ice-hockey player scores three goals in one game, what is it called?

A: A hat trick

Global Fun

Test your knowledge of trivia relating to world geography with this multiple-choice quiz. Read each question and see if you can select the correct answer.

1. Which is the only U.S. state that borders only one state?

A. Rhode Island
B. New York
C. Maine
D. Vermont

2. What do the people of Korea do the first week of a new year?

A. sing songs to welcome the New Year
B. fly kites and release them to carry away bad luck
C. bake cupcakes to sweeten the new year
D. give presents to one another

3. Still standing today, the Bridge of Eggs was built in 1610 and was made of mortar and the egg whites of more than 10,000 eggs. Where is the bridge located?

A. Peru
B. Indonesia
C. Costa Rica
D. Argentina

4. Which is the largest body of fresh water in the world?

A. Lake Superior
B. Lake Geneva
C. Lake Como
D. Lake Michigan

5. Which city is the largest in the U.S. in terms of land area?

   A. Salt Lake City, Utah   **C.** Juneau, Alaska

   B. Dallas, Texas   **D.** Billings, Montana

6. In Brazil and China, which of the following is considered rude to do?

   A. chew gum   **C.** wear sneakers

   B. smoke cigars   **D.** whistle

7. Which does the nation of Indonesia have more than 13,000 of?

   A. species of birds   **C.** species of trees

   B. islands   **D.** mountain ranges

8. Established in 1565, which is the oldest continuously settled city in the United States?

   A. Plymouth, Massachusetts   **C.** Saint Augustine, Florida

   B. Philadelphia, Pennsylvania   **D.** New York, New York

Answers

1. (C)	3. (A)	5. (C)	7. (B)
2. (B)	4. (A)	6. (D)	8. (C)